James McLain

D0753803

FUNNY BUSINESS

Prentice-Hall International (UK) Limited, London
Prentice-Hall of Australia Pty. Limited, Sydney
Prentice-Hall Canada Inc., Toronto
Prentice-Hall Hispanoamericana, S.A., Mexico
Prentice-Hall of India Private Limited, New Delhi
Prentice-Hall of Japan, Inc., Tokyo
Prentice-Hall of Southeast Asia Pte. Ltd., Singapore
Whitehall Books Limited, Wellington, New Zealand
Editora Prentice-Hall do Brasil Ltda., Rio de Janeiro

Ken Berryhill

FUNNY BUSINESS

A PROFESSIONAL GUIDE
TO BECOMING A COMIC

A SPECTRUM BOOK

Prentice-Hall, Inc., Englewood Cliffs, New Jersey 07632

Library of Congress Cataloging in Publication Data

Berryhill, Ken.
   Funny business.

   "A Spectrum Book."
   Includes index.
   1. Comedy.   2. Comedians.   3. Comic, The.   I. Title.
PN1922 B47 1985   792.7′028′02373   85-6404
ISBN 0-13-345406-1

A Spectrum Book

Printed in the United States of America

1 2 3 4 5 6 7 8 9 10

ISBN 0-13-345406-1

Editorial/production supervision by Rhonda K. Mirabella
Cover design by Hal Siegel
Manufacturing buyers: Frank Grieco and Carol Bystrom

To my wife, Mary M. Berryhill,
my sons K. Wayne and Dale A. Berryhill,
and to the memories of my parents,
Clyde A. and Lucille C. Berryhill,
and my sister Zephna Berryhill.

CONTENTS

1

Basic Information, 1
Why Do People Laugh?   Historical Aspects
Types of Humor   Terms   Naturally Funny, or Actor?

2

Major Areas of Comedy, 15
Clown   Pantomimist (Silent)
Pantomimist (Recordings)   Standup Comic (One Liners)
Standup Comic (Monologues)   Sketch Performer   Impressionists
Master of Ceremonies   Magicians   Jugglers

3

Comedy Material, 31
Use of Others' Material   Hire a Writer   Write Your Own!
Buy Ready-Made Comedy Material   The Public Library
Jargon and Clichés   Blue Material   Filing Your Jokes
Memorizing Your Routine   Length of Your Act

4

Appearance, 53

Makeup   Costumes   Props

5

Gauging Audiences, 69

A Variety of Audiences   Prior to Performance
During the Performance   After the Performance

6

On Stage/On Camera, 81

Audience Interplay   Timing   Use of Music
How to Handle Hecklers   Use of Cohorts

7

Stage Fright, 95

Lost Talent   Personal Experiences
Conquering   Coping

8

Being Funny for Money, 109

Beginning   News Releases   Portfolio   Brochure
Applying for Jobs   Auditions   Some Good Advice
Is an Agent Really Necessary?   Is a Personal Manager Really Necessary?
Is Union Membership Necessary?   Does Comedy Pay Well?

Index, 125

FOREWORD

by Phyllis Diller

A young gentleman asked me to sketch in a bit of "knowing" about the Tragedy of Comedy and, I'd like to add the term, the Comedy of Errors.

You've got to realize that when all goes well, and everything is beautiful, you have no comedy.

It's when somebody steps on the bride's train or belches during the ceremony that you've got comedy. The contrast of great pomp makes comedy even funnier.

There is a certain bag of tricks that comedians use. They are simple techniques for making a human being look ludicrous.

A person standing straight and tall, with eyes ahead, head high, is not funny.

Now, picture the court jester of the ancient kings, usually a hunchback with a big nose. These are still the trappings of comedy. Think of Groucho's crouched walk with eyes rolling, the ugly noses in the business, girls with mouths a little too big (like Carol Burnett and Martha Raye), or eyes made to look too big, like Carol Channing's.

My stance is crouched over, slightly hunchbacked, feet pointing in opposite directions. The cigarette holder is used to show hostility. I do little beats with it at the end of phrases to punctuate some ugly things I've said.

Therefore, all comedy is based on tragedy, either minor enough to be talked about now, or ancient enough to be spoofed. In other words, you don't joke about someone who died yesterday.

Most people seem to feel that you either are a comedian/comedienne or you are not. They consider the ability to make other people laugh to be an inborn trait, a congenital talent that requires no outside training or influence. But the author of this book, Ken Berryhill, thinks otherwise, so he approached Memphis State University with the idea of actually *teaching* people to be comedians and comediennes. Result: a class taught by Ken each year, this book, and his graduates on stages and before cameras at this very moment.

This book, the embodiment of his entire course, enables the author to reach far beyond the strict limitations of his classroom and touch countless individuals who have fantasized about entering the wonderful world of comedy. He assures each of you that, talented or not, if you listen to and practice what he says, you *can* and *will* become a professional comedic entertainer.

Ken Berryhill is the perfect comedy instructor for two reasons. First, he has been entertaining for almost fifty years on radio, television, and stage and knows numerous clowns and comics on a first-name basis. In addition to being a comic disc jockey, he has been a clown, standup comedian, pantomimist, and master of ceremonies. Second, having been a professor at a major university, he knows how to systematically arrange material so that it may be taught in a manner that will be best absorbed by the students. He knows what to convey and how best to impart that knowledge.

I am not joking when I tell you that this book just may change your life.

PREFACE

This project began as a book, but before I progressed very far I realized that it was instead a letter—a lengthy letter to one person. I found myself writing to some faraway, unknown aspiring comic, someone going through what I went through many years ago. I know too well the contradictory feelings of desire coupled with the frustration of not knowing how to get started in such an appealing, yet far from run-of-the-mill, business.

And so I guide this individual step by step through a process that is more complicated and difficult than anticipated by the novice. I first lay groundwork in the form of discussing what makes us laugh and the historical aspects of comedy. Then I exhort the student to determine introspectively whether he or she is naturally funny or will have to resort to acting. Both can succeed—but differently.

The numerous areas of comedic activity are revealed so that the student may survey the wide variety of openings available. Best of all, the student will realize that lines may be crossed to enable him or her as a performer to blend two or more forms into a winning combination. Sources of comedy material are discussed, as well as the importance of professionally done makeup, costuming, and comedy props.

Because I feel that any performer must adapt to his or her spectators, I devote an entire chapter to analyzing any given crowd. Interplay with members of the audience is discussed, as is timing, use of music and cohorts, and how best to handle hecklers.

Because one of the biggest hurdles for the beginner is stage fright, it is discussed in full with the idea of teaching the neophyte how either to conquer or to cope. Finally, the course is wrapped up by telling the new comic how to get started: where to get jobs, union membership, the value of booking agents and personal business managers, and just how much financial compensation can be expected at both the bottom and top of the profession.

My intent has been to write in a clear, easy-to-read style so as to produce a sought-after guide for all age groups that will also be valued through one's comedy career as a handy reference guide.

Acknowledgments

The following have, directly or indirectly, aided in the production of this book: David Brenner, Phyllis Diller, Wink Martindale, Anne Meara, Don Rickles, Jerry Stiller, Danny Thomas, John Bartholomew Tucker, Steven Wright, Peggy Michel, Jack Adkins, Thomas Brooks, Berkeley Davis, John Langley, Bobby Lawson, Diane Mandolini, Dawne Massey, "Pidge" (Eugene Pidgeon, Jr.), Ray Sauer, Evelyn Stanford, Maxine Street, Beth Sullivan, Lon Viar III, Dot Williams, Frank Taylor, Mary Taylor, Carol Neal (photographer), Milton Goldman, Lou Viola, Marty Klein, Ingrid Vanderstok, Jeff David Thomas, Thomas H. Landess, Dennis Deas, Jeff Minton, Stephanie Kiriakopoulos, Laura Likely, Rhonda Mirabella, Jack E. Dunning, Sr., Mary M. Berryhill, K. Wayne Berryhill, and Dale A. Berryhill.

Finally, special thanks to my editor, Mary Kennan. After all, this book was really her idea.

FUNNY BUSINESS

1
BASIC
INFORMATION

I have long boasted that "I can make a comic out of anyone," and I mean it. I have never, however, suggested that all my products will be equally funny or successful. People vary when it comes to innate talent, stamina, and intelligence. But if you will assiduously study my directions step by step and apply them faithfully, I can assure you membership in that august society of elite entertainers: the comedians and comediennes! Step one is to mold the proper mental attitude by analyzing laughter and comedic history and to determine introspectively your natural abilities or lack of same. Your expressed interest in comedy is indeed a tribute to your obviously high I.Q., since all comedic activity requires intelligence for its production, reception, comprehension, and enjoyment. Furthermore, the field has a rich heritage that covers all of recorded time and may possibly extend back to the very first stirrings of mankind's reason.

Why Do People Laugh?

Exactly what is laughter, and why do we laugh? We don't really know. It has baffled scientists and psychologists for ages. Strangely, we don't confine our laughter to funny sayings and events only. We often find ourselves emitting the unearthly sound at the sight of something that, in itself, is pure tragedy. For example, when you witness a mishap wherein injury will in all likelihood result, you find yourself laughing and not knowing why. You will get the "giggles" when in a situation which, by its very nature, dictates that thou shall not giggle, such as a church service or an ultrasolemn wedding. You will even go into uncontrollable and hysterical laughter when under extreme stress. The answer to this singular phenomenon lies in a file drawer labeled "The Unexplained," but the important thing is that people *do* laugh, and, more important for you, they truly enjoy laughing. Therein lies the reason for the comic's existence.

You should be mindful of the fact that although a variety

Jack Adkins, shown backstage, is a recording star and comedy actor. His off camera life is totally divorced from his comic TV characters. (Photo courtesy of Carol Neal.)

of things can cause laughter, these vary from person to person, culture to culture, and from one time period to another. What is funny to a fourteen-year-old may fall flat when perceived by a forty-four-year-old. What is hilarious to a Chinaman in Hong Kong may be totally misunderstood by a Frenchman in Paris. And a joke that may have brought down the house in the 1700s might produce at best a smile when heard by a modern person. For instance, if you search through periodicals of a hundred years ago you will find joke sections, true, but most of the jokes of that period were simple riddles or plays on words. "When is a door not a door? Answer: When it is ajar!" That must have been a knee-slapper then, but it rates only a groan today. You should never lose sight of this concept, constantly revising and updating your comedy material to satisfy your varying audiences and the changing times. Stay up to date.

Laughter begins extremely early in life. Babies smile, gurgle, and chuckle well before they learn the language. Some people will laugh uncontrollably when physically tickled. Others will look daggers at you and make vague references about their intentions of doing you bodily harm or summoning the police. We elevate ourselves in nature's realm by feeling that we alone in the animal kingdom enjoy humor. This is ridiculous. Did you ever watch kittens or puppies at play? They and countless other young creatures are nature's little comics, cavorting and mock-attacking to the obvious delight of both their companions and onlookers. In short, comedy is purely innate. It is so interwoven within the fiber of creation and so basic that it is inseparable from life itself. It is as basic as thirst, as inborn as breathing. Laughter and life are synonymous.

Is it, then, just possible that laughter is *not* a product of a well-developed higher intellect that has evolved far above other animals and is, instead, a *lack* of development in the cranial area? Is it perhaps another strong link with the animal world? Could it be a form of retardation? It's just a thought.

It has been suggested that laughter is perhaps a physical or mental defense mechanism—nature's way of maintaining equilibrium in a world where stark realities often cause anguish beyond endurance. The supposition is that laughter causes some chemical release that tends either to strengthen or to nullify the brain, enabling nerve cells to either prepare for the problem or shut down and let the storm pass without enduring suffering. There have even been reports of people banishing serious illness through the use of a single medication: laughter. Until further research wins me over, however, I think when ill I will still consult my physician instead of a comic.

Historical Aspects

We can historically trace comedy to ancient Grecian dramas, the earliest being centered around simple ridicule with little or no discernible plot. A gradual evolution moved dramatic comedies into higher realms of complication and sophistication, hopefully producing increasing volumes of laughter.

Who is to say who was the very first standup comic? We might be safe in assuming that it was some long-forgotten cave man a few millennia into the past who, after a meal of me-

A normally calm Jack Adkins explodes on stage as rock star "Rick Stagger." (Photo courtesy of Carol Neal.)

dium-rare mastodon meat, rose to relate to other cave dwellers exactly what happened during the hunt earlier in the day. Through gestures and exaggerated actions he related a serious occurrence in a humorous manner, much to the delight of his prehistoric audience. He was, no doubt, asked to repeat this show many times, became very popular, and was handsomely paid with extra food and personal attention unlike anything he had known. Others, seeing the advantages, began to emulate him and showbiz was born.

Perhaps the first recorded ancestor to our modern comics was the court jester. According to historical accounts, he was a combination buffoon, magician, and wit. Reportedly, many of his comedic comments were highly intellectual in nature, and there is even evidence that courtly decisions were at times influenced by his remarks.

As the years rolled by, we had tellers of tall tales, renderers of humorous sketches, monologists, dialecticians, parodists of melodrama, minstrels, and comic song artists. Comedy material appeared in the early years of audio recording with the Uncle Josh (Cal Stewart) series, Nat M. Wills, Bert Williams, the teams of Gus Van and Joe Schenck, Ed Gallagher and Al Shean, and Joe Weber and Lew Fields, to mention a few.

As in all areas of natural and human phenomena, the evolutionary process of comedy continues. Video and digital recordings, lasers, satellites, cablevision, computers, and other advances in electronics, coupled with ever-changing cultural ideals, guarantee that comedic trends are changing even as you read this. Be aware of the advances and stay flexible throughout your career so that you may remain popular with your audiences and always aware of the rich history of entertainers who preceded you.

Types of Humor

Joke. This is a vague, broad term which includes virtually anything from humorous stories to one liners, the latter being one or two phrases or sentences that in themselves form the complete joke with punch line.

Humor of situation. Laughter is often provoked by incongruity, the combining of two or more items that seem to belong miles apart. A ragged and dirty person attending a formal dinner party is an obvious example. In addition to incongruity, and often coupled with it, is humor of surprise, which occurs when the brain is suddenly given a situation that is totally unexpected.

Humor of words. A pun is simply taking a word of one definition and suggesting that it relates to some other word or definition in a manner that renders the entire line humorous. Punning is often put down as being the lowest form of humor, an accusation born of the fact that puns are so easily contrived and often appear in conversation with neither forethought nor intention. The charge may be understandably correct for the majority of puns. Well-developed and carefully-written puns, however, can be effectively used to get a point across and, in the hands of an expert gag writer, can be extremely funny. One word of warning: No matter how funny your pun is, I guarantee that the audience will always groan after you deliver it. Don't let that deter you. If the pun is really funny, use it. But use puns as you would spices on food, sparingly.

Spoonerism. This is the transposition of the beginning letters of words and the general corruption of word forms to develop a new language or a form of double-talk. If done well and delivered professionally the result can be most entertaining. Examples include the phrases "Thinkle peep" (people think) and "Pee Little Thrigs" (Three Little Pigs). Use this type of humor sparingly also. A heavy dose of this can drive an audience up the wall and out of the auditorium.

Hyperbole (exaggeration). This is when a situation is so blown out of proportion that the resulting effect is humorous. Example: "Boy, is that guy thin. He's so thin that if he stands sideways you can't see him."

Repetition. This is often called the buildup to the punch line. A situation that in itself has no humorous overtones is repeated a number of times until a well-defined punch line brings the entire picture into mental focus and the result is funny. A series of words is often used instead of full situations. This technique is in common usage and most long jokes use repetition as their foundation.

Comparison and contrast. This is humor derived from either combining two or more ideas or situations that are similar (comparison), or that are totally dissimilar (contrast).

The list could go on, since there are variations on each of these and different shades of definition. But my purpose here is to briefly acquaint you with the basic types so that they become malleable in your comedic hands for use in either joke writing or performance—or both.

Terms

Burlesque. The word comes from the old Italian *burla,* meaning jest or ridicule. This began as a form of parody but evolved over the years into a type of variety show punctuated with clown-like comics, sexually suggestive jokes, and strippers. Many of the old silent movie comics did their basic training in burlesque theaters. Many current television shows are direct descendants of the old burlesque shows, and are, like their predecessors, most entertaining. The burlesque comics are a unique breed and are often highly paid. They are masters of timing.

Farce. This is generally satirical and has a most improbable plot, interspersed with highly unlikely occurrences. Many early silent movie comedies were simple farces. Many clown acts are farcical. While basically ludicrous, it is a highly developed form of comedy, being carefully planned and masterfully executed. It is generally athletic in nature and performers often stay away from it because of the difficulties of effective presentation. Slapstick comedy falls under this heading.

Irony. This is an unexpected yet strangely justified end result of a given situation. Example: A man chases some kids with a garden hose only to trip over the hose himself and end up thoroughly doused, while the kids run away laughing and dry.

Mimicry. This is mimicking or imitating a person, animal, or thing, usually with exaggeration. Impressionists are masters at this. Record pantomine also falls into this category.

Parody. This is a humorous alteration of a widely known song, play, story, or event, with the purpose of calling attention to the foibles of an individual or group.

Sarcasm. A sarcastic utterance is one made with the intention of belittling, hurting, and ridiculing an individual or idea. It can be raised above the level of brutality by tone of voice or demeanor, but any intended humor is usually lost by the per-

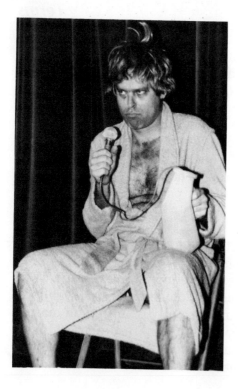

A master of mood changing, Jack Adkins goes into his "World's Oldest Living Judge" routine. (Photo courtesy of Carol Neal.)

fidiousness of the remark. Example: "That's a nice swimsuit you have on. Do you like it better than the ones in style this year?" Funny to onlookers, but devastating to the intended recipient.

Satire. This is an attempt to ridicule with the motivation of improving, the idea being that by calling attention to wrong-doing or foolishness, people will come to their senses and make the necessary changes. Most political cartoons are satirical.

Wit. Unlike other forms of humor which rely on abnor-malities, wit is intellectual in nature and is often based on learned allusions. It can be very effective, but is difficult to produce since its success is dependent upon the audience's educational background for full comprehension of the chosen allusion. It is often confined to select cultures, classes, age groups, and ethnic backgrounds.

Naturally Funny, or Actor?

Some people have a congenital ability to evoke laughter simply by their natural appearance, demeanor, or quick-witted verbal talent. This is a tragedy beyond words for those who cannot tolerate being laughed at, but a blessing to those who glory in the attention and reactions they create. On the other hand there are people who, while not being naturally funny, are talented enough actors or actresses that they can play the role of comic to the point that the viewing public would not be aware that it is merely contrived. These people present routines that are carefully planned, studied, and devised, but it does not mean that they are less funny. They can be just as funny as the natural comic, but with greater effort in both preparation and performance.

My reason for including this seemingly worthless bit of information is actually very important. It is vital that you recognize early in your career into which category you fit. Are you naturally funny, or do you find that when you entertain

Stan Laurel and Oliver Hardy worked well together despite the fact that Stan was a naturally funny man while Oliver was an actor from start to finish. The latter could turn his comedic talent on or off at will.

you have to act the part of someone who is very distant from your own personality? If you are naturally funny, then breathe a sign of relief, for your job will be far easier. You can wow any audience by simply getting on stage or standing in front of a camera and being yourself.

Let's look at the other side of the coin, however, before you give up a promising career. A good actor or actress can go far beyond the natural limitations of a person who relies only on natural "funniness." A good actor or actress will have the world at his or her feet. Am I, then, talking out of both sides of my mouth, praising both the naturally funny entertainer and the actor whose routine is all put on? Yes, I praise them both, for they each have their own sphere in which to rule supreme. If you must resort to acting, so be it. But don't overlook the fact that there are varying degrees of natural funniness. The absolute best comic is therefore the often-found combination of a naturally funny person who can also act. If you fit this category, success is guaranteed.

As a personal observation based partially on remarks from others in the field, I consider the following to be naturally funny people who are, or were, also talented actors: Tim Conway, Bob (Elliott) and Ray (Goulding), Buddy Hackett, Stan Laurel, Steve Martin, the Ritz Brothers, Red Skelton, Rip Taylor, and Robin Williams. These are presented merely as examples, and names left out are done so due to space limitations. I could literally fill the book with the names of talented comics.

"Dr." John Langley is another comic who can turn it on or off at will. When he is clowning, it is all an act. (Photo courtesy of Carol Neal.)

Conclusion

Knowing the historical background of comedy is vital so that you may adequately comprehend what went into the building of comedic entertainment. By reviewing the past you can not only appreciate it but also be better prepared to handle the present and future. Suffice to say that things will change, so be ready to adapt as necessary. Knowing the types of humor and terms gives you something to build on and enables you to effectively communicate with your peers. Furthermore, you are now aware of a factor so often overlooked by novice enter-tainers: the difference between the natural performer and the actor, and how the two may be combined to create the ideal comic. You are now in proper mental synchronization to move to a higher level of instruction.

2
MAJOR AREAS
OF COMEDY

T oo often an entertainer new to comedy has tunnel-vision and completely overlooks the broad spectrum of the field. As a beginner, your time will be best spent in reviewing major areas of comedy. This may introduce you to some new ideas and form a part of your basic training by establishing that, while you cannot be all things to all audiences, you can vary and embellish your act in order to attain the highest levels of this wonderful profession. The full import of this chapter's contents will not become fully apparent until its conclusion. So join me as we explore various major comedy areas, all of which are open to you.

Clown

In the comedy realm the clown is something extraspecial. This performer is singular and highly respected by his peers. Clowns generally are males or females with painted faces and outlandish costumes who perform stunts and tricks to the delight and hilarity of the audience. We usually think of these buffoons as entertainers of children, but few adults will pass up a chance to watch them go through their paces.

They date far back into history, easily to the court jester, and have probably shown less change over the years than any other form of entertainment. They appeared in circuses very early, but in those days they talked, sang, and played musical instruments. Later the talking and singing disappeared to the point that today most clowns are pantomimists, though some are not adverse to using fireworks and sound effects. They are given credit for being the stars of circuses. I often feel, however, that they are relegated in some shows to being mere comic relief, or punctuation, between the main acts of a circus or parade. I cannot praise these outstanding people enough and I shall never grow too old to enjoy watching them.

I have known several of the truly great circus clowns and have had the rare opportunity of discussing their art with them. It is a highly specialized profession to which many may aspire, yet few may receive the highest accolades. I have been a clown on television, stage, and for private parties, and I can attest to the fact that it is pleasureable yet exacting and exhausting work. It is purely and simply athletic.

If you select this area you will be limited by the bounds of your own energy and inventiveness, and the more outlandish contraptions and routines you can devise the better. Cars and any other form of vehicle on wheels can be employed. You can fool the crowd by pointing into the air at something that isn't there. You can balance six to eight bars of soap on your chin (empty soap wrappers all connected by cellophane tape!) You might play with an invisible ball, occasionally tossing it into the audience (they will not only catch it, they will throw it back.) You could endeavor to step on a nonexistent bug that eventually goes up your pants leg. A horn complete with air bulb could be hidden under your costume to be tooted at will with your elbow. There are thousands of other possibilities that you can originate just by putting your mind to it.

The circus arena and the parade are but two of their stages. Clowns often work independently for private parties (usually birthdays), store openings, special retail sales, shopping centers, and special civic events. I recently visited a well-known tourist attraction that is so popular that waiting in line is dreaded by all. To ease the pain of delay, the astute managers hired clowns to keep the crowds entertained. It worked! Clowning is an excellent way to break into comedy, since job openings are bountiful.

Pantomimist (Silent)

This is another highly specialized form of entertainment. It is the acting out of some activity in total silence. There are those who modify the idea and use background music timed to punctuate particular moments in the sequence, and those who employ sound effects, but a pantomimist generally works in utter silence. This entertainer can be extremely funny, though quite often we find that the act is more artistic and thought provoking.

The chances are that you will not select pantomime as a lifelong career, but I advise you to explore the field and practice it. If nothing else, you will develop an artistic appreciation for it and will find it to be excellent basic training for the areas into which you finally settle. Silent pantomime is excellent discipline for all entertainers. It establishes in the mind a sense of organic attention, an outward appearance or action that is contrary to fact. For example: On stage you may pick up what the audience perceives to be a cardboard box full of books, yet in actuality the box is completely empty. You must convey to the spectators an illusion, through organic attention, that looks exactly as though you are lifting a heavy object. Even your voice must strain when the lifting begins. Practice this until you can fool anyone with it.

Here are other beneficial pantomimic exercises. Practice them straight at first, adding comedy elements later on.

1. Taking out, lighting, and smoking a cigarette
2. Skiing (snow or water)
3. Playing golf, tennis, and so on

4. Stacking books, plates, and the like
5. Getting into, starting, and driving a car
6. Pulling a loose thread from a coat or sweater
7. Fishing
8. Typing
9. Washing a big dog
10. Building something with carpenters' tools

All of the above, and innumerable other situations, can be done to great comedy effect by exaggeration of movement, facial expressions, and a general reduction of the chosen action to its ludicrous basic components.

Pantomimist (Recordings)

Imagine a baritone voice coming from the throat of a petite comedienne, or a soprano note pouring from the mouth of a burly comedian. Always a hit is an act that includes record pantomime.

To pantomime a recording you simply mouth the words while the recording is playing. You actually say nothing. You can also pretend to play the various instruments and add facial contortions and bodily movements to augment the hilarity of it all. Some comics look for records that, in themselves, are funny. Others can select virtually any recording and devise a funny presentation. The act can be embellished by fright wigs, crazy costumes, blacked-out teeth, colorful makeup, and an endless array of props.

Many young comics begin in this area, and here is how to perfect your routine. Select the record—old, current, top pop, country, foreign, it doesn't matter. Either on the record player or on tape, play the song over and over until you are ready to stop or drop. While it is playing, stand in front of a mirror with your face well lighted and mouth the words until you have developed a perfect synchronization with the record. You do not want your lips to lag behind the lyric nor rush ahead of it. It must look exactly like the words are emanating from your mouth. When this has been done to your satisfaction, give it the acid test. Videotape yourself, close up on face at first, pantomiming the record. When you have reached lip-sync perfection you can concentrate on introducing props, facial actions, and body movements.

Don't forget this: You are not limited by the record itself. You can edit a number of records and sound effects together on tape and create whatever the mind can conceive. You can even include sections of blank tape during which you speak carefully chosen jokes or phrases, or even sing yourself. Be creative. Don't be shy about trying new things for fear that they won't go over. Try them out on your audiences. If an idea does fail, simply drop it from the act.

I once saw a night club comic who ended his regular joke-telling routine with a surprise. Suddenly, all of the lights went out except for his special black light. All we could see were his specially madeup face and gloves as he pantomimed a rousing and laugh-provoking record. It was great.

An added personal note: When I was starting out and wanted to win an amateur show, I always used my old record pantomime act. I always won first prize.

Standup Comic (One Liners)

The general picture is that of a lone entertainer in the spotlight with a microphone. While onstage, that person is the whole show. The standup one liner comic delivers a series of very short laugh lines, often with little continuity or no continuity whatever. The jokes are literally one line in length, though at times they are actually collections of several brief phrases or sentences. The comic often machine-guns these gags so fast that you don't have time to decide whether they are really funny or not. Some comics run along with one liners, then drop in a joke or funny short story that requires background information.

These entertainers are most often found in night clubs,

though they are not limited to that medium, and they are popular almost beyond belief. Some have international fan clubs and are literally idolized by the members, who are not adverse to traveling hundreds of miles to catch their deities' live performances. They are sought after by show producers in such places as Las Vegas and Atlantic City and can command salaries of astronomical proportions. Television gives the top comics prime spots on a regular basis. Many wind up with lucrative movie contracts.

It is the good life if you enjoy travelling and are not allergic to the tobacco smoke and alcohol consumption that seems to go with night life. While the hours are strange it is hardly labor beyond endurance, and if you stay off of television you can go for months, even years, without changing your routine. You will have a plethora of leisure time, will dine well and have excellent living quarters (usually), and you will see the world.

If it is all that great, why isn't everybody out doing it? Because few comics are that good. You will not start off in the manner I just described. To the contrary: You will spend years before building up a following that marks you as a top comic, though there are some very rare exceptions who make it literally overnight.

These standups all seek to be original and as different from others as possible. Different approaches are employed, various ploys are explored. Some use props, some use music. Some banter with the audience while others seem little aware that it is there. To be succinct, the standup comic fits a neat classification, but his or her act can be modified a thousand different ways.

Standup Comic (Monologues)

This is the same as the one liner standup comic except that this individual generally stays away from one liners and prefers a string of jokes or stories, usually related and in a logical sequence, or with reasonable transition from one subject to another. This is termed a "monologue." It is an old entertainment technique, but it is perennial. Since these areas overlap, it is possible to do a monologue of one liners.

Sketch Performer

This is something quite different from the clown or standup comic. A sketch performer appears in what may be described as very short plays, running five to ten minutes in length, and packed with humorous and hilarious situations and punch lines. While it is excellent training for any aspiring comic, it is very difficult, if not impossible, for some. You have to be an excellent actor or actress to pull this off with success. Many can't seem to cross the line. Some excellent sketch actors fail as standup comics, and vice versa. Many television shows have been built around a series of funny sketches, as with burlesque. It has been said that a sketch actor is only as good as the

Dawne Massey, Evelyn Stanford, and Ray Sauer display the wonderful camaraderie between comics. Other performers can calm your nerves, aid you in last-minute preparations, and evaluate your act. (Photo courtesy of Carol Neal.)

material provided. I disagree. I feel that a real actor can take the worst possible sketch material and *make* it funny.

Impressionists

Always a crowd pleaser is the comic who does impressions of famous people. Keep in mind the sharp difference between an impersonator and an impressionist. The impersonator endeavors to recreate and copy a personality as exactly as possible. The perfect impersonator will talk, walk, sing, and wear clothing just like the subject to the point of being that person's double. The problem for us is that this is not always funny, nor is it always intended to be. On the other hand, the impressionist gives his or her impression or caricature of the subject with humorous distortion and exaggeration.

You may wish to specialize on singers only, or do impressions of other comics. Then again you might choose famous political figures or movie stars, or wisely decide to mix them up, selecting those who are currently popular. Whatever your decision, you must spend far more rehearsal time than average in order to emulate the voice and mannerisms of your subject. Listen to recordings of your subject, or repeatedly watch the

John Bartholomew Tucker. Former TV announcer on "Candid Camera" and noted for TV commercial voice-overs, he is the master of all masters of ceremonies. John has always made excellent use of his carefully chosen comedic addenda. (Photo courtesy of John Bartholomew Tucker.)

Wink Martindale. This famous recording artist, TV gameshow host, and public speaker punctuates all of his performances with pertinent comedy lines. He is a master of ceremonies par excellence. (Photo courtesy of Wink Martindale.)

individual in person or on electronic reproductions. Do this until you can adapt to their style, adding your comic changes, with ease.

Master of Ceremonies (M.C.)

Off and on in your career you will be asked to be the master of ceremonies (M.C.) for a show comprised of many acts. Your routine, with all of your gags and props, will be featured, but it will probably be scattered throughout the program between the other performers. It is hard work because you are on stage or on standby during the entire show, but it is a good change of pace and can be a lot of fun if the acts are talented and the audience receptive.

Here are a few brief tips for a master of ceremonies.

1. Do your homework. Glean in advance as much information as possible about both the performers and the audience. Prepare particular gags just for this special occasion.

2. Talk with each performer before the show, making sure you

know exactly how names are to be pronounced, in what order, and the correct title for the act.

3. See if any act needs anything special added to its introduction.
4. Be respectful of all other participants in the show. Give respectful introductions unless an act has prior knowledge and gives approval for a sarcastic or seemingly degrading remark on your part. Ascertain this first, because while you may think it funny, they may consider it insulting and debasing, and will never forgive you.
5. Respect the planned time limits of the show. Keep an eye on your watch, or have someone give you time cues. Many otherwise excellent variety shows have been ruined because they ran on ad nauseam. Keep your introductions brief unless there is reason to stretch, such as filling in time while a set is changed behind the curtain.
6. Above all, remember that you are not the star of this show. You are merely the catalyst, the thread that produces a continuity between otherwise unrelated acts. In short, you may be the frosting on the cake to be sure, but the other acts form the cake itself. You will not make any extra money by trying to convince everyone that you are Charlie W. Bigdeal.
7. Finally, as you should throughout your career, carefully get names and permanent addresses of everyone with whom you perform. Keep a file for future reference and contact the performers periodically. Your cards should indicate when and where you worked together. This will become invaluable in later years and will aid everyone concerned in future job procurement.

Magicians

How about comedy magicians? You haven't been entertained until you have watched these funny people. Basically they are excellent magicians (usually) who have developed a flair for clowning during their performances. Sometimes they have pointless tricks that go nowhere, while they assault you with an endless banter of gag material. At other times they impress you with expensive equipment and surprise you with baffling feats of magic all wrapped in humorous trappings. Combining magic with humor is an excellent device, and the comic magician is high on my list of fine entertainers.

Jugglers

How about jugglers? No comedy here, you say? You are wrong. Admittedly this is a rare breed because of the long hours required to perfect and maintain the art, but these people bring home the money.

There are three ways to learn. One is to be taught by another juggler. This is the ideal, but jugglers are hard to come by. The second is to read or buy a book on juggling and meticulously follow each direction very carefully. The problem here is that the novice always wants to move ahead to phase two before he or she has completely mastered phase one. The result is

Multi-talented Bobby Lawson makes use of numerous abilities to wow his audiences. He sings, plays guitar, tells jokes, and does impressions. (Photo courtesy of Carol Neal.)

frustration, disenchantment with the art, and a misguided feeling that you are not talented enough. The book is tossed aside or left to gather dust, and a promising career crashes before takeoff. The third way is to teach oneself. Talk of going about something the hard way, this is it! But it can be, and has been, done. A classic example is the young man who, during idle moments in the retail store where he was employed, began picking up and tossing into the air whatever items were at hand: rolls of toilet paper, ash trays, cans of food, and so on. Before long he said goodbye to retail sales and gave the big hello to showbiz.

And is it possible to tell jokes while juggling? Yes.

Other Areas

By now you should be awakening to the fact that any form of entertainment can be turned into a comedy act with great success. How about music, singing and dancing? Surely you have seen comedy acts built around one or more of these areas. The story is oft-repeated of someone who is a good musician, or good singer, going virtually unnoticed among the myriad others of their ilk until he or she becomes a comedy musician or singer. The chances are excellent that you are multi-talented to begin with, so mastering two or more instruments and singing will present no great hurdle.

Combination Performers

The beginning comic may, by this point, experience bewilderment. With so many areas to choose from, how can a person choose the best one? While you may settle on one area early or later in your career, I advise you to consider two or more. I want you to become a combination performer, able to weave comedy in and around several basic entertainment modes. Believe me,

A true combination performer, Bobby Lawson, at work. (Photo courtesy of Carol Neal.)

the audiences will appreciate this far more than the character who hits the stage, stands in one spot, and for twenty to forty-five minutes hurtles half-funny jokes at them. Begin by dropping in a bit of juggling here, some singing there, perhaps a few chords on the banjo, then a brief magic trick or two. You will enjoy it. The audience will tell their friends about you. And the money will roll in. Isn't that what it's all about?

Conclusion

You can see that the areas of comedic activity are best characterized by the word "variety." It is like being in a dream world where you view endless fields of diamonds, rubies, gold and silver coins, and exquisite jewelry creations, all of which are available to you and can be combined anyway you choose to bring everlasting career satisfaction, happiness, and wealth. The information in this chapter is a good basis for your show business education and should help you feel more comfortable with your peers. It should also assist you in building an act that will make even your competitors sing your praises. Toward this end, you are now ready to focus on specifics in your personal comedy routine.

3
COMEDY
MATERIAL

Somewhere in a long forgotten backstage area eons ago, someone muttered a statement that has been repeated countless times: "A comic is only as good as his jokes." But, let it be understood that a comic's success is by no means totally dependent upon the successful delivery of funny stories. He or she should also employ all available techniques: Facial expressions, gestures, props, makeup, pantomime, and humorous situations. I am nevertheless compelled to devote the next few pages to a very important facet of comedic entertainment: the acquisition of jokes, how to properly file them for future reference, and methods employed by professionals in memorizing comedy routines.

By simplest definition, a joke is any utterance that produces laughter on the part of the person hearing it. And though that seems simple, it becomes a complicated matter for the professional entertainer who constantly needs fresh and original material. Many a budding career sputters out when the original act begins to wear thin and the laughter becomes almost imperceptible: New jokes are needed. Fresh material should replace the time–worn gags used too long and too often before the same audiences.

Follow my directions and you will never run out of gag material. You need to acknowledge early in the game that this will happen to you if you don't prepare ahead. The answer is to have an abundance of standby material ready at the snap of your fingers. This requires a great deal of work on someone's part and a modest monetary investment. You also need to educate yourself as to the sources of comedy material and how you may draw from them.

Use of Others' Material

Copyrighting a joke is comparable to trying to strike a match on a cake of ice: Not impossible, but close to it. Humorous books, sketches, and plays are put under copyright all the time, but many jokes have been around since ancient times and do not qualify for such legal protection. These are in the public

Jerry Seinfeld. After only a few years, Seinfeld has gone from "open mike" auditions in small New York comedy clubs to over a dozen appearances on Johnny Carson's "Tonight Show," the Merv Griffin and David Letterman shows, and the major showrooms of Las Vegas and Tahoe. And he has accomplished this remarkable feat without the aid of crazy hats, toys, or other props. Articulate about his brand of comedy, he also dismisses insult and put-down humor as pointless. "We're not in a battle," he says of his relationship with an audience. "It's not a competition, is it?" Rather, Seinfeld's material is wry and smart. With a soft-spoken, unhurried and truly elegant subtle style, he makes the wittiest observations on our modern culture that get the truest response from an audience—the very loud laughter of recognition. (Photo courtesy of Jerry Seinfeld.)

quip. When someone shyly approaches you to listen to a few of his original jokes, don't say "Go 'way, kid, ya bother me!" Listen to him. He just may be the answer to a funnyman's prayers.

The finding and hiring of writers can be done via advertising. Local papers can be used, but it is usually accomplished through the various trade papers in both entertainment and writers' journals. It works both ways: Comics advertise for writers and writers advertise the fact that they are available. Advertising agencies and college faculties are also excellent sources of writers. Be warned that gag writing is highly specialized and the fact that someone is a published writer in one area (such as novels) does not indicate that he or she can change and start writing jokes. I have found, however, that good speech writers are usually also good gag writers.

Write Your Own!

One way to write jokes is to brainstorm: Jot down whatever comes to mind and carry it in any direction that the brain directs. Knowing that I would begin writing this particular chapter today, I decided while shaving this morning that I would brainstorm a joke. For some unknown reason my mind delivered the image of a goldfish. If anything is unfunny, it is a goldfish. But I decided to have a go at it. I thought of fishing. I thought of a platter of fried goldfish. I thought of a talking goldfish. But I couldn't head it for a punch line. Finally, I had it. I exaggerated the goldfish in my mind until it weighed ninety-five pounds, which put me in the realm of the ridiculous. After modifying the wording numerous times, I finally polished the joke to it's finished form:

> For a pet I have a ninety-five-pound goldfish. He sleeps at the foot of my bed. It's a waterbed.

Funniest joke you ever heard? Of course not. But it *is* a joke. Could every comedian use it to great effect? I don't think so. I think that it would appeal only to those with weird approaches.

Audiences have loved Danny Thomas for years. One reason is his constant supply of socko comedy material. (Photo courtesy of Danny Thomas.)

But the important thing is that this morning I wrote an original joke, and you can, too. And you should try to write at least one per day, though most days you will come up with far more.

My students frequently back off at this command, saying that they possess absolutely no talent for writing original jokes. But I always prove to them that they do. True, this peculiar talent varies from one individual to another. But everyone has the spark and all you have to do is fan it into a flame. How many times in class, at a show, on a bus, train, or subway have you had a wisecracker near you? Some of those characters are truly good entertainers. They comment on whatever the action is and often get off a wisecrack worthy of headliner gag writers. You see, wisecracking is gag writing. If you had written down every wisecrack you had thought up since the third grade, you would probably be rich by now selling them to television and night club comics.

I generally give my students a starter and let them build a joke from that. For example, if I give the topic *dog,* it is a vague starter. But if I give *dog smoking a pipe,* I have done most of their brainstorming for them, since I have suggested new areas such as ecology, tobacco, matches, and visions of dogs sitting

The best way to write gags is with one or more comics. You can brainstorm for ideas and receive fast reactions to your newly born routines. (Photo courtesy of Carol Neal.)

around chatting while puffing on pipes. Starters aid you immensely, and they are everywhere. Pick up today's newspaper. Virtually every article and feature is a starter for a gag. The same goes for current news and shows on television. You will never lack for gag ideas, never.

Student writers go through three distinct mental phases when faced with the inescapable assignment of writing an original joke. Let's say that they are given the vague and basic starter of *automobile*. Phase one is that after some pondering, they come up with a totally unoriginal joke that they already know about an automobile. Prodded to try harder, they enter phase two, which is to take an old unoriginal joke and change it around to fit the category of *automobile*. Finally, after a bit of cajoling on the part of the instructor, they will go into phase three and come up with a truly original automobile joke. While some never quite seem to make it successfully into phase three, most do and are amazed by their latent talents and abilities. The three phases do not disturb me as a teacher. They are the natural mental steps necessary to gear the mind up to the level

Comedy writer Robert Orben, author of forty-six books of professional humor, wrote his first book at age eighteen. His works are used as basic sources of humor by most professional entertainers and public speakers. After writing for the Jack Paar TV Show in New York, he was in Hollywood from 1964 to 1970 writing for the Red Skelton TV Show. He also wrote for Dick Gregory for six years and edited Dick's first two books: From the Back of the Bus *and* What's Happening? *(Photo courtesy of Robert Orben [Robert Orben Comedy Center, 700 Orange St., Wilmington, De., 19801].)*

of originality. This exercise seems difficult, but is surprisingly fun.

At this point let me turn *you* into a gag writer. Simply follow my directions step by step. First, the hard part: Find a quiet room in which to concentrate, making sure that there are no distractions. Second, get a pen and plenty of blank paper. Third, practice writing jokes for the starters below. Be as original as you can, but put down whatever comes to your mind. Take as much time as you like, and take breaks as often as you feel the need.

1. A pizza
2. Marijuana, drugs

3. A television set (or show)

4. Some current news event

5. A nudist camp

6. Baldness

7. A Drunk (or drinks, drinking, bars, and so on)

8. A major holiday

9. It was so cold (hot) last night _____ .

10. He/She is so dumb that _____ .

11. He/She is so fat/thin that _____ .

12. I am writing a letter to the President of the United States. How do you spell _____ ?

13. I wouldn't say that my wife is a bad cook, but _____ .

14. I wouldn't say that my husband is lazy, but _____ .

What is the first thing you do after you dream up an original gag? Write it down! You may think that you will remember it, but an hour later it is gone forever. Write it down, and indicate that it is original. I maintain a special file which contains nothing but my original jokes.

Worthy of mention at this point is something that has happened to every gag writer at some point in his or her career. I once thought up an original gag, wrote it down, recorded it in my file, and used it in my act. About a year later, while thumbing through some old joke books that I had had for years, I came across my original joke. I hadn't created it at all. I had read it years before and forgotten it, and my brain spit it out as original. This strange thing will happen from time to time, but try to avoid it at all cost.

Buy Ready-Made Comedy Material

If hiring a personal writer seems impractical or impossible, and if writing your own jokes strikes you as laborious or tedious, there is an alternative: Purchase jokes from a comedy supply firm. There are not a lot of these around, and addresses are

Robert Orben and former President Gerald R. Ford. In 1974 he became President Ford's speechwriter, and in 1976 he was appointed a Special Assistant to President Ford and Director of the White House Speechwriting Department. Robert Orben has written an average of twenty-five jokes per day for thirty-seven years. (Photo courtesy of Robert Orben [Robert Orben Comedy Center, 700 Orange St., Wilmington, De., 19801].)

hard to come by unless you live in a very large metropolitan area. Librarians can aid you in procuring addresses that cannot be found in trade papers.

These firms specialize in comedy material for speakers, standup comics, special convention presentations, and the like. They charge nominal fees and the jokes are generally good, though you will have to pick, choose, and edit to satisfy your particular needs. Most of them offer full books which are separated into categories and alphabetized, making it easy to find in seconds a gag on almost any subject. In addition, some offer monthly or quarterly newsletters, with fresh, up–to–date gags on current events and personalities. You must usually subscribe to these for a minimum of one year, a worthy investment for the beginning comic.*

One obvious source of jokes often overlooked by newcomers is the local bookstore or book sections of department stores. These places usually have a variety of joke books in stock, or they can show you lists and order whatever you want.

The Public Library

Don't forget your public library in your quest for comedy material. Before seeking aid from the attendants there, first consult the card catalog under various cross sections: jokes, gags, humor, comedians, entertainment, public speaking, comedy, and so on. If unsuccessful, tell the attendants exactly what you are looking for and their aid will be invaluable. Library jokebooks are often outdated, but that does not mean that there are no good jokes there. While it is unlikely that you will want to build an entire act based on what you find in a public library, it is not impossible.

Jargon and Clichés

When writing or researching jokes, watch out for jargon which may cause an otherwise funny joke to be either misinterpreted or misunderstood. Jargon is the use of words or phrases that are peculiar to a particular group of people. With computers, for example, there is terminology which may sound like a foreign language to the uninitiated. A joke using terms like "software," "bytes," and "bits" may get a laugh from the computer crowd, but fall flat on the ears of anyone uneducated to such words. Use jargon only when appropriate.

Then there is the cliché, a stereotyped word, phrase, or expression which is trite, overused, and unoriginal. I won't tell

*Just one of the many excellent firms producing gag material is: The Comedy Center, 700 Orange Street, Wilmington, DE 19801.

A wealth of comedy material is available in your local libraries. Careful research and methodical filing on your part are necessary. (Photo courtesy of Carol Neal.)

you that you should never use clichés, but rather that you should use them only when the joke is completely lost without them. Even then I question their value.

Blue Material

Blue material refers to jokes that run all the way from mildly suggestive to extremely vulgar, and early in your career you will be torn between whether or not to insert some of this into your act. Your employers may insist on it, but you may feel uncomfortable for any number of reasons, including personal moral code, religion, family influence, or just plain embarrassment. What to do?

Students constantly ask me "Do I have to be dirty to be funny?" The answer is no. Numerous famous comics have lasted for years on television without so much as a sexual innuendo. Do your act the way *you* want to do it and limit yourself to the audiences you desire to entertain, and you can still reach the heights.

As for myself, I feel that anyone entertaining the public should be broadminded and tolerant and should give audiences whatever the current trends in comedy are. But let me qualify that. If the insertion of a dirty word is truly hilarious, or if the joke is not a joke without it, I will have to vote for its insertion. Too many comics, however, pour out endless mouthings of filth for shock effect only: This I vote against. If you think that the audience will love and remember you more for a series of four-letter gutter words, you are wrong.

Don't be afraid of suggestive insinuations or sexual allu-sions, but remember that you are in business for yourself, so you can include or exclude whatever suits your fancy.

Filing Your Jokes

Let me start with the wrong way to file jokes for future use. This is what I call the idiot method. I know how wrong it is because it was the way I began and I have regretted it for many years. The idiot method dictates that you should jot down only a couple of words to remember the joke by, writing it on a news-paper, book margin, or perhaps a scrap of paper to be thrown into a small box or file marked simply "Jokes." Result: Within a few months the couple of words are totally meaningless and the joke is lost forever. Within a short period of time the newspaper or book from which the joke came cannot be found. Within a year the joke file is bulging with valueless scraps of paper in no particular order, so that a search for material on a given subject is a boring, if not hopeless, task.

The correct way to file jokes is this. Buy a supply of index cards. I prefer three-by-five-inch unlined, white cards, but that is a matter of personal choice. This size suits me best because it will hold virtually any joke (typed) and fit neatly into my pocket for rehearsal or referral. In the upper left corner indi-cate the category into which the joke fits. The original joke about the ninety-five-pound goldfish, for example, might be categorized under "Pets." Then type, print, or legibly write the joke as completely as possible on the card, using the back if necessary. You will save time and space by using either standard shorthand or a devised shorthand of your own.

But don't stop there. Your work is far from over. Put the same joke on two more cards, labeling the following categories in the upper left corner: "Waterbed" on one and "Fish" on the other. For some jokes you will find that they fit into five or more categories, while others only two or three. This way you have a cross-reference that takes a little time at first, but one that makes life easier for you later on when you are researching your own files to put a routine together on specific topics.

From an office supply store purchase the proper size boxes or drawers in which to place these cards. Under no circumstances should you attempt to stack them on a desk or table or wrap a rubber band around them. Your act is your business, so be businesslike from start to finish.

This is the simple method. But you can carry it further if you like. For example, in addition to the category method above, some performers use a color-coding system that enables them to spot at a glance a certain type of joke. They color the upper center edges of each card. Green means "okay for family audiences." Orange means "borderline risqué." Red means "hot stuff for adult audiences only." Colors or numbers can be used as your needs direct.

Ideally, your joke file should be fully computerized.

Memorizing Your Routine

Once you have your carefully chosen storehouse of jokes and have molded them into your routine, what next? You must now memorize the entire sequence, and for a required twenty to thirty minutes on stage or camera, that is a formidable task. You wonder how the pros do it as you watch and listen with wonder as they click off gag after gag with no discernible loss of place or memory. Following are their secrets.

The easiest method is by the use of cue cards. This is routine in television studios but extremely rare before live audiences where there are no TV cameras. The cue card is a

large piece of white poster board on which is written whatever is to be said by the performer. Large felt-tip pens with black ink are used, or black paint and narrow paint brushes. The words are written very large so as to be easily read from a distance of up to twenty-five feet or more. Another term for these cue sheets is flip cards, and they are often jokingly referred to as idiot cards. They can be mounted on or near a television camera, but they are most often held up near the lens by a member of the production staff and turned or changed as dictated by the copy itself.

Another method is the electronic prompter. While watching political conventions and other large presentations on television, you have probably noticed rods to each side and slightly forward of the person speaking. On each rod is a tilted piece of clear glass. From the audience side you can see through the glass, but the speaker sees his speech projected from below and reflected. As he speaks, the text printed in very large letters moves steadily upward, keeping the spoken line always centered. There are variations of this, some using actual television screen monitors. Some prompters are mounted directly on cameras so that the performer, while reading the script, is looking directly into the lens and, thus, the eyes of the viewer.

Although the cue cards are handy, they are laborious and time-consuming to prepare, and any change in your routine necessitates new cards being printed. And it goes without saying that the electronic prompters, although the ultimate in present-day sophistication and convenience, are far too costly and bulky to be practical for most individual performers. So the one-comic act is left with either reading the jokes from cards or a script, or literally memorizing the entire routine. In more than fifty years, I have seen only two comics read their jokes from hand-held cards, and only one did it with any fair amount of success. I simply do not advise doing that, for it marks you as a rank amateur.

You are left with what seems to the newcomer in the business the impossible task of memorizing a mile-long string of jokes and keeping them in the correct order. But you can easily do it! The secret is mnemonics, which is a strange-looking word derived from Greek that in the broad sense refers to improving or assisting memory. Let's be more specific. Let's use the word in the sense of supporting the memory by use of visual associations. If you have a long, complicated joke or one that is extremely abstract, think up some concrete visual representation which, whenever thought of, reminds you of the joke or at least of the opening line. Usually if you can come up with the opening line you can easily continue.

These visual images should be as bizarre, eye-catching, and unforgettable as you can make them. Use strange and incongruous sights! Use sexual allusions! Involve visions of people who are performing far out of the realm of normal daily activity (people flapping their arms and flying . . . a man walking on his ears . . . someone being led on a leash like a dog). The idea is that although you may forget the joke itself, the bizarre image will stay with you far longer and help you remember the joke.

It is vital that these fantastic mental pictures be designed to someway tie in directly with the joke. When possible, they should come directly from the joke itself. Otherwise, you might be on stage and easily remember a zebra in a helicopter but have no earthly idea of which gag it is supposed to remind you!

Once you have these weird associations stamped in your mind, then for continuity you must place them in the correct order in a known geographic location. This could be a room in your home, your car, the room in which you are performing, one of your old classrooms, a street, a campus, etc.

Here is both an example and an exercise. I will make this easy for you by suggesting the mental association for the following four jokes:

1. My wife has a complexion like a peach: Yellow and fuzzy. (Image: Huge overly ripe peach)
2. Her teeth are like the Ten Commandments: All broken. (Image: huge set of false teeth)
3. She has a basketball nose: always dribbling. (Image: bouncing basketball)
4. I wouldn't say that she is tough, but she puts her earrings on with a staple gun. (Image: hand holding staple gun)

At this point you are probably saying, "Cheez, I can remember the gag easier than the image." But the images will come into clearer focus when I put them in the following geographic location. Let's use your bedroom. Pick a wall. Any wall. On that wall (or on a piece of furniture against it) imagine a huge overly-ripe peach, which you should immediately associate with joke #1. Then, to move the mind from #1 to #2, picture the peach flying over to the second wall and being chewed by a huge set of false teeth (Ah, there's your mental cue for joke #2). Next, the teeth spit the chewed peach to your third bedroom wall where a bouncing basketball (your cue for joke #3) trounces the already mutilated peach. Finally, peach juice squirts through the air to cover a staple gun (your final cue) hanging on the fourth wall.

You may understandably complain that this is a lot to go through just to remember four one-liner jokes and suggest that one might simply memorize them. You would be correct if only four jokes were involved, but when you appear before the audiences and camera, you will be dealing with from fifty to 200 jokes and even much higher when you become an Atlantic City or a Las Vegas headliner. Trust me! The answer is mnemonics! You should study and practice it until it becomes an integral part of your being.

Once you have used a certain geographic location for your mental cues, don't use it again for several months after you have stopped featuring that particular routine; otherwise, you will confuse a new image with an old one and blow your act.

Let's do one more exercise. I will provide the gags. *You* dream up the associated images and place them in the geographic location of your choice. I have selected unrelated gags just to make it hard for you:

1. I'm like a mosquito at a nudist camp. I don't know where to begin. (Image:)
2. I bought some pills guaranteed to bring back my teenage complexion. Now I have pimples all over my face. (Image:)
3. What does a short order cook say when he is sick to his stomach? Answer: "One pizza coming up." (Image:)

4. Ah, my poor Uncle Henry. Last night he put his false teeth in backwards and bit himself to death. (Image:)

Once it is all implanted in your mind to your satisfaction, close the book, go into another room, and see if you can repeat all four jokes with no pauses between them. Let a day go by without reviewing the jokes on the printed page and, believe it or not, you will recite all the gags in perfect order!

Finally, there is the system of literally memorizing your entire act verbatim. Nothing wrong with that if you have the time and want to run the risk of either totally forgetting the routine or losing your place with no planned method of getting back on the track. Use this method if you choose, but don't come crying to me when you make a fool of yourself on stage. After you have done a particular routine enough times, however, it will be cemented into your memory for a long time to come and memory devices will become unnecessary.

Length of Your Act

Just how long a one-person comedy routine should last always bothers the beginner. One wants to put on a good show but wants to be careful not to stay on stage to the point of wearing out the welcome. There is no pat answer. It will often be dictated by the particular show in which you are appearing or by the owner of the club into which you are booked, but I can give a few guidelines.

Unless under a television or movie time restriction, never perform less than five minutes. Normally you will be expected to fill around twenty, so always be prepared for that. On the other hand, if you are the headliner in a big club, it is not unusual to expect an hour to an hour and a half. The latter will not come until much later in your career, so you have plenty of time to work up to that gargantuan task. In the meantime, think mainly in terms of twenty to thirty minutes maximum.

By the way, any old pro will tell you: It is far harder to be funny in a restricted five minutes than in twenty or more.

Conclusion

Remain conscious of your continuing need for new laugh lines. Be constantly aware of the modes at your disposal of acquiring fresh joke material, routines, and ideas. Once you have them, *write them down,* cross-file them, and develop your own system of mnemonics so that your brain will become a virtual storehouse of comedy ready to back you up on any stage before any audience at any time. Have you noticed? You are becoming more professional already.

4

APPEARANCE

F ar too many amateur entertainers feel secure in the careful selection of their comedic niche, and they feel equally secure if they have socko material. And they simply let it go at that. The real professional is very conscious of the equally important areas of facial makeup, costuming, and props. To ignore these would be comparable to building a house with no windows or an automobile with no wheels. Your entire act is a combination of many different elements which, when blended carefully, give to the audience a lasting impression of professionalism.

Makeup

The amateur comedian can usually be spotted by the obvious lack of makeup. Some novices simply forget to put it on. Others don't think that they need it. And then there are those who remember it, and know the need for it, but shy away from its use because of their ignorance of how to acquire or apply it to best advantage. One might assume that females take to stage

Former Ringling Brothers, Barnum & Bailey circus clown Pidge (Eugene J. Pidgeon, Jr.) made the transition to standup comedian. He learned early in his career that applying makeup is a slow and painstaking process if the results are to be effective. (Photo courtesy of Carol Neal.)

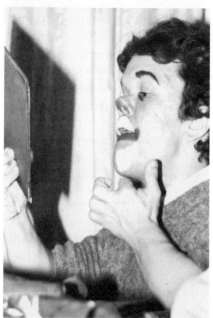

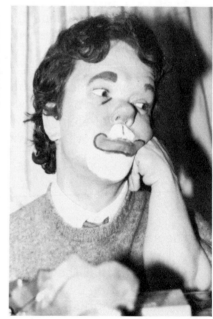

makeup naturally, since they are programmed by their mothers from an early age in the use of powder, rouge, and lipstick, but this is not always the case. The application of makeup for stage and television lighting is quite different from the method employed for everyday personal contact in the office, classroom, meetings, social events, church, and gatherings in general. There are professional comics who do use drugstore cosmetics throughout their entire careers. Some defend it as being lower in cost. I question that. Some say that there is no difference between professional makeup and that purchased at a local cosmetic counter. And others simply got used to the makeup they had on hand at the beginning of their careers and never changed.

To the beginning comic I strongly recommend that you begin with professional makeup, and here is the way to start without a huge outlay of money on products that you may later find don't suit you. Contact a professional entertainer (not necessarily a comic), and ask to use some of his or her makeup for purposes of experimentation. Offer to pay for this privilege. Explain that before investing in your own supply, you wish to find out what is best for your face shape and your skin's tonal quality. Seek to experiment with that person present, asking his or her advice. This might be done with two or three entertainers to glean as many valuable opinions as possible. You should not be shy about approaching them because show people, with all of our peculiarities, generally enjoy helping newcomers get started in the business.

Don't make the mistake I made when I was twenty-one. I was entertaining with a twenty minute record pantomine act: No gags, just one pantomine after the other. A *tour de force* for both me and the audience. Up until that time, it had always worked without makeup. After winning an amateur show, I lucked into a week's work in a burlesque house when the theatre owner needed someone to fill a spot left vacant by an entertainer suddenly taken ill. There were no private dressing rooms in the old theatre. I shared a room with an old comic who professed to have been one of the original Keystone Kops in silent movies, and the master of ceremonies who, within a few short years, was to become one of the top standup comedians in the business. While alone in the dressing room one night, I noted some professional makeup before the mirror and decided to experiment without permission. It belonged, as it turned out, to the extremely hot-tempered master of ceremonies who didn't have to look far to find the culprit (who had makeup all over his face.) I shall spare you what he said to me, but I will tell you that he announced to the theatre owner that either I or he (the M.C.) had to leave the show. The good-natured owner placated him by pointing out the fact that he would be working with me for only one week, so things settled down. It was my fault, and I was sorry for the incident. All I had to do was ask if I might use some of the makeup. Chance never threw us together on the same bill again, and I regret it for he was, and is, a very funny man—on stage.

When you experiment with makeup, don't ignore anything on your face. Watch for moles, scars, peculiar eyebrows, shape of nose, eyes, heavier than normal beard, and so on. Instead of hiding some feature with makeup, you may wish to highlight or spotlight it. If you have a big nose and it will aid you in being funnier, make the nose even more prominent. On the other hand, if you may have small or otherwise insignificant eyes, you may wish to bring them out by the use of shadowing or blacklining. You may be disgusted with a mole or birthmark, but it just may become your trademark. The first time I met actor Richard Thomas (John Boy of the hit television series "The Waltons") was in a theatre lobby after a preview showing of his early and virtually forgotten movie *Cactus in the Snow*. While watching the movie, I thought that the birthmark on the cheek had been added for visual effect. But while chatting with him I was surprised to see that the mark was natural. He said that it was his decision to never cover it with makeup. You will agree that his birthmark became his trademark. But remember that Richard Thomas is a serious dramatic actor, not a comic. You should constantly ask yourself: Will this make me funnier? If so, go with it. Highlight and amplify those features that make you a better comic, and carefully subdue those which distract from your important and difficult business of getting laughs.

Comedienne Dot Williams gives credit to makeup and costuming for much of her success. She always applies her own to transform herself into characterizations that evoke laughter the moment she appears on the stage. (Photo courtesy of Carol Neal.)

A special word to those people with unusual complexions. Judge your makeup requirements based on your complexion, not on someone else's. For example, you may have exceedingly light skin or a natural tan. Or you may have inherited an olive complexion. Once, during filming at Paramount Studios in Hollywood, I heard a makeup man say that the olive complexion is the real challenge for the professional markup artist.

It is you and your associates who must, by trial and error, finally arrive at the best possible look to be funny. But watch out for the big error: Too many beginning performers get close to a mirror under a single incandescent bulb, or a fluorescent tube, and work out their makeup to their satisfaction and then wonder why they fail to progress in the business. Although you may look great from two feet away, the audience will be seeing you from several feet to several yards away and under different lighting. You will simply not appear to them as you appear to yourself in the dressing-room mirror, but solving the problem is simple. By using a video cassette recorder, you can see yourself as the audience sees you: same distance, same lighting. That mole that you are so proud of may literally disappear to anyone beyond the fifth row. Those big dark eyes may be just black blobs to someone fifty feet away. A professional comic will work with a video tape recorder time and again to get a new bit of business or a new makeup idea worked out. Get to it.

Costumes

What to wear? If you have observed the comedy scene long enough, you are well aware of the various cycles it goes through. There was the outsized costume (hat too small, pants too large) that was common in the late 1800s and early 1900s. Some, like Charlie Chaplin, used the tramp outfit, literally picking up whatever clothing might be at hand, regardless of size or style. These were true comic characters in that they did not look at all like anyone in their paying audience, but they did tend to ridicule a hapless segment of society so often laughed at by the public. The spectators could then have it both ways: They could laugh at the jokes and routines while also laughing at those less fortunate than themselves. These old costumes were clownlike, despite the somber colors and common styles, but smacked of being amateurish in that they gave the appearance that some young person rummaged through an attic and found bits and pieces of old clothing that didn't fit and wore them in lieu of originating and paying for an innovative outfit. In short, those comics were cheap. But once the trend started and it became obvious that people would pay to see a man in a sloppy suit, the trend continued unabated for many years. We now look upon the old pictures of such costuming as quaint and antique and question the cultural taste of audiences of that day.

As this trend gradually disappeared, comics began to move to even less innovative costuming: They appeared on stage or camera in street clothes. How many comics have you seen with a business suit and tie? This is funny? George Carlin, early in his career, appeared dressed either in tuxedo or business suit, but he later changed with great success to a "hippie" appearance (blue jeans, sloppy sweater or T-shirt, unkempt hair, and a slight growth of beard). Whether or not he looked good is not the point. The important thing is that he looked different and was eye-catching. And then there is Steve Martin who comes on stage with a white suit. Different enough to be funny.

Widely known for outlandish costuming are members of the country music business. The outfits are usually takeoffs on western garb, but no self-respecting cowboy would be caught in public or private in such an array of sequins and rhinestones. I once questioned a famous country music singer/composer about the often gaudy apparel worn by his colleagues. He answered with a shrug, "It simply comes with the territory. The idea that no one wants to watch an entertainer who looks like the man next door is a valid one." I concur. Thus I advise all novice comics to place as much attention on costuming as on makeup and jokes. That shirt, that dress, that sweater, just may be a famous trademark someday! *Your* trademark. Select your outfit very carefully. Try out various arrangements on

The versatile Dot Williams performs one of her unique characterizations. (Photo courtesy of Carol Neal.)

"Dr." John Langley finds his comic character coming forth when makeup and props enter the picture. (Photo courtesy of Carol Neal.)

video tape. Finally and most important: Don't be afraid to change when you see that either (1) it isn't working, or (2) it is outmoded.

Here is an exercise for you. For the next week or two carefully observe every comic you see on television, in movies, or live performances. Write down what is worn for the shows, then analyze them carefully. Did what they wear make them funnier? Did the costumes distract from what they were trying to accomplish? Could they have dressed better or more professionally? Did it seem that they had given no thought to dress? Use your analysis to help direct your own future. Profit from their errors while picking their brains for ideas.

Props

What are a comic's props? By "prop" I do not refer to something placed under or against something to support it, though by a twist of the imagination the definition just might be appropriate. The word *prop* in the world of showbiz is jargon for the word *property* and refers to any article or object used by the comic while performing. Costumes and scenery are not included, though they rightfully fall within the definition. I refer, therefore, to material things you might employ by wearing, manipulating, or otherwise displaying that will enhance your performance by punctuating your already funny verbal material and your personal comic antics. How about the everpresent cigar used by numerous comedians over the years? Remember Henny Youngman's always present but seldom-played violin? Morey Amsterdam's occasionally-played cello? Phyllis Diller's extralong cigarette holder? Woody Allen's black rimmed glasses? Shelley Berman's perennial cigarette? One might justifiably question whether these devices actually added to comic effect or were merely easily identifiable trademarks. You might recall my explanation of what a prop *isn't* and say that the cigar, musical instrument, or other item might be merely a nervous affectation of the performer's, something to lean on while doing the act.

My contention is this: The beginning comic should care-

All of Dot Williams' routines are completely original. (Photo courtesy of Carol Neal.)

fully investigate and become fully aware of the variety of comic props and be ready to use them whenever and wherever effective to enhance the spoken material, to establish a trademark, or to use as a security blanket while performing.

We have just passed through a phase of standup comics who used no props and no special costuming. Using these devices would have associated the comics with the oldtimers, and they wanted to be up-to-date. The pendulum keeps swinging, however, and the new comics are using every device they can get their hands on to call attention to their acts and to move into the higher elevations of this unique and enjoyable profession. Puppets are being made out of shoe boxes and handheld tape recorders. Some current puppets are mounted on the hand, using the fingers as legs. Ridiculous hats are making a comeback. Bizarre coats and dresses are seen. If it works, use it. Equally important: If it doesn't work, never use it again.

Where does the beginning comedian seek out and acquire props? One good place is the proverbial trick or fun shop. Every city of reasonable size has one or more. Drop in, browse around, and make sure that they know what you have in mind. Attend estate sales, flea markets, and garage sales. If an item looks like it might have possibilities, and if the price is right, buy it and work it into your act wherever possible. If it fails, your investment was small and of no consequence. Later, when you are a more sophisticated and wealthier performer, you can devise and have your props made to order.

Don't overlook electronic equipment that can be fed into the existing PA (public address system) of the club or auditorium you are working. Pantomiming records is an old, but still effective, method of entertaining, and by changing the record speeds and expert editing you can blow an audience's mind. Use multimedia whenever possible: slides, movies, sound organs, stroboscopic light, black light, lasers, telephone answering machines, video cassette recorders, even smoke alarms. Think about it: There are hundreds of comedy bits that can be associated with the small list of electronic items just mentioned.

As for myself, I wouldn't be caught on stage or in front of a television camera without any array of props, or gimmicks, as I

Props are where you find them. Don't overlook any sight gag that might enhance your act. Comics Diane Mandolini, Lon Viar III, Berkeley Davis, and John Langley plan for a comedy showcase. (Photo courtesy of Carol Neal.)

call them. Here is just a partial list of gimmicks I have acquired and used to good effect over the years:

- Two-foot-long cigar
- Squirting cigar
- Large can of peanut brittle (actually contains three long spring-snakes that pop out when the can is opened)
- Black wig
- Bright orange wig (I made this myself by removing the handle and dying a mop bright orange, then trimming to fit my face)
- A variety of hats—black derby, cowboy, bill cap, formal top hat, flat porkpie hat, soft straw with brightly colored band and rim turned up (much too small for my head), and a construction hardhat which I have painted and repainted a variety of colors
- Ukelele
- Fake mustard dispenser (long yellow string comes out when squeezed)
- White gloves (extra large)
- Small windup animal that goes wild when released

- Bicycle horn (long and curved with a big rubber bulb)
- Fake ears (larger than normal)
- Balloons
- Masks (old man, Batman, and so on)
- A variety of ties with ridiculous colors and designs (one even lights up)
- Glassless eyeglasses with large fake nose attached
- Spiked ball attached to a chain and black handle (scares the living daylights out of an audience which refuses to laugh at my gags)
- Large fake spider (often slightly hidden on my sleeve)
- Fake eyeballs (one set crossed and another reminiscent of Little Orphan Annie)
- Kazoo
- A variety of magic tricks
- Lifesize plastic roach (I often come on stage with this dangling from my lower lip)
- Pair of huge bloomers (thirty-six inches wide)

Comedienne Dot Williams, off stage. (Photo courtesy of Ken Ross.)

The list goes on, but I think you get the idea. Do I use all of these every time I perform? Of course not. Some gimmicks remain put away for a year or more until needed. It is vital that you, as a beginner, understand that a prop is to be used only when and where effective. These gimmicks should be considered as merely the punctuation marks for your entire act.

Highlight your jokes and antics with carefully chosen and discretely used props, and you are putting the finishing touches on an act that is moving from the amateur level to the coveted realm of professionalism.

Conclusion

Your single object when you perform is to elicit laughs. Don't lose sight of that obvious but often ignored fact. Take great care in selecting and applying the facial makeup that will make people smile or laugh the moment they first see you. Some comics add mugging or gurning by twisting the face, pouting the lips, widening the eyes, contorting the mouth, flaring the nostrils, and so on, to great effect. Other comics work deadpan. But no professional comic works without makeup. It is an area of great importance, as is your selection of what you will wear and how you will wear it. Will a hat upside down get a laugh? If so, do it. Will one red and one blue glove make an audience giggle? If so, wear them. And constantly review your available props, adding new ones and deleting those which have become passé. Finally, remember to use a video cassette recorder to constantly review your makeup, costume, and props in order to polish your act until you are America's top comic.

5
GAUGING
AUDIENCES

Years from now, long after you have become a headliner in the big casinos and on television, you may pick up this book again and whimsically thumb through the pages, remembering your early days in showbiz. And when you come to this chapter you will laugh, skipping over it hurriedly, muttering to yourself, "I certainly don't need to read that again." By that time you could rewrite the chapter for me and perhaps add many pages based on your own experiences. My purpose here is to make the fledgling comic aware that each audience has its own personality and to show how to anticipate and gauge those differences and adapt the act accordingly. Simply put, what one audience will laugh at another will not. After a joke, one group may come forth with a belly laugh, a second with a chuckle, while a third may literally not comprehend the joke at all. You must consider such factors as the average age of the audience members, the income level of the majority of them, and their educational status to mention just a few important areas. Much of your work, as you have already learned, must be done prior to performance. You must be conscious of this and be able to anticipate and plan carefully for the particular audience you are to face.

A Variety of Audiences

Make up your mind early that it will be impossible to develop only one routine for use before all audiences. It won't work. You need not only a series of different types, but also a flexibility that will enable you to change the act, while performing if necessary. It isn't easy, but a real pro can handle it.

Let me run through brief examples of different audiences you may face from time to time, pointing out reasons why they will not all appreciate the same jokes.

Stiller and Meara. In both comedy and serious acting roles, Jerry Stiller and Anne Meara appeal to a wide variety of audiences. (Photo courtesy of Jerry Stiller and Anne Meara.)

Young children. You must obviously speak distinctly and slowly. You should smile or look pleasant at all times. Remember that they will not comprehend sarcasm. They will take everything you say literally, so be careful. Make concrete statements as opposed to abstract. Do not use vague or learned allusions: They won't understand them. But children are very good at visual images if adequately described, and they love slapstick situations. When adults hear of someone falling down stairs, they may laugh at the mishap but the laughter will be tempered by thoughts of broken bones, pain, doctor bills, ambulances, emergency rooms, and insurance claims, not to mention lawsuits. But the children? They will think of none of this. They will simply see a big person tumbling down stairs and that will appear funny to them. Children are a delightful audience and usually very respectful, though not always attentive. Their attention spans are very short, so have changes built into your act. Move from a funny story to a funny magic trick to a bit of comedy juggling, and so on. And don't plan to stay on stage long.

Early teens. Individually, I love children in this age group. Collectively, they make for the absolute worst audience for a comic. They are energetic, intelligent and outgoing. They love life. They love to entertain. And there's the problem: *They love to entertain.* We make a mistake by saying that people in their early teens want to be entertained all of the time, for the stark reality is that they constantly seek crowds so that they may do the entertaining. Get a couple of hundred of them under one roof and you have what might be best compared to an insane asylum. Put a good comic on stage before them and they will invariably heckle, constantly wisecrack to those around them, and throw on stage whatever is handy. Long ago I told my manager, "No more early teen audiences."

School groups. How is this group different from the first two audiences? The school audience is usually composed of a variety of ages, with resultant peer pressure to tone down the rowdy elements. Furthermore, they are being monitored by one or more teachers, and in some cases, the dreaded school principal.

Church groups. Ages in this group vary. You might be asked to entertain at a church banquet attended by entire families, or you may be invited to perform before a particular age group. Most church audiences are very receptive and polite, but blue or risqué material is forbidden. The adults usually have a high school education and many have at least attended college. Some have college degrees. Occupational status and financial standings vary with the surrounding community, size of church, and denomination. Church audiences are always very receptive to your performance and will let you know it. It is one of the most genteel groups you will face.

Family reunions. Your reception will vary depending on whether or not you are a member of the family. This is hardly the world's most attentive audience since they are getting together with people they seldom see and prefer to gab and gossip instead of paying attention to your act. The routine should be kept family-style clean. The best way to win them

Phyllis Diller has the audience in the palm of her glove from the moment she appears on stage. (Photo courtesy of Phyllis Diller.)

over is constant audience participation, even to the point of having a number of them come on stage. A word of warning: Don't insult or ridicule anyone.

Civic and service clubs.   Quite often these audiences are composed of adults of a single sex, so you may face a large room filled with middle-aged women or men. It will vary with the particular affair: regular meeting, special Christmas dance, and so forth. These are generally very good audiences for the beginning comic. They are tolerant of both mistakes and lapses of memory, and know what it feels like to face an audience. You will have their sympathy, their good wishes, and, if you are any good at all, their laughs. For the most part these clubs are made up of well-mannered, law abiding citizens who have the interest of their community at heart and will give you their full support. Don't ever miss an opportunity to entertain these people.

College crowd.   It is difficult, if not impossible, to put a tag on this age group. It is full of surprises. I often think that they themselves cannot predict with any degree of accuracy their next mood change. A lot of your success with them depends on

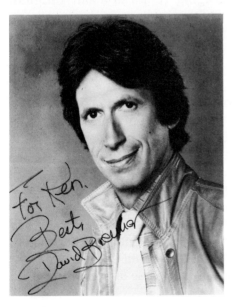

David Brenner, a master of comedic delivery, timing, and gauging audiences. (Photo courtesy of David Brenner.)

what time you come onstage. If it is an afternoon seminar session in the library they will receive you one way, but at night in a fraternity house or an on-campus concert, the reception will alter considerably. This age group is not adverse to ingesting things that "expand their minds," so they might receive an entertainer one way early in the program yet react quite differently an hour-and-a-half later. Despite what I have just said, I consider the college crowd one of the absolute best for a comic. They will accept any type of material, their feelings cannot even be dented, and the age of the comic makes no difference to them. Feel complimented when invited to entertain the college crowd.

Country music fans. Forget the wornout stereotype of a barefoot farmer with one tooth missing and a hound dog at his side. That was the Hollywood image from ages past. Present-day country music fans are often well-educated and affluent. They are a comic's dream for they will accept virtually any joke of any age except the extremely vulgar. As a matter of fact, they seem to thrive an old jokes. You can make fun of the audience, the band, the auditorium, almost anything except religion. Do not make disparaging remarks about religion, churches, or preachers in front of this audience unless you have one foot outside the door and the car motor running. But if they love you, you will never have more loyal fans. You will be richly rewarded beyond your wildest expectations.

Night and supper clubs, discos, and so on. Here I am lumping together all latenight places that feature entertainers because the audiences vary only slightly, depending on geographic locations. The audiences here consist mainly of adults who are imbibing alcohol. While I personally do not drink, this is my favorite audience. Their blood-sugar levels are as high as possible and they are ready to have fun. You will seldom, if ever, bomb out with this crowd, though they may not remember your name the next morning. Risqué material is not only permitted, it is expected. There is often a band to bring you on, back you up, and take you off, and you will have use of excellent sound equipment in most places. Your first performance in a night-spot will be an experience you will never forget.

Bars.   I separate the bar audience from the above classification because of a noticeable difference in attitude. These people come in mainly to drink and the entertainment is secondary. Reactions to your gags will vary around the room. Some conversations will not stop when you begin, and there will be at least one totally obnoxious drunk who will be hellbent on getting you off of the planet. Usually, however, these are pleasant places in which to appear and the work is much easier than in the big rooms or auditoriums because the bar is toned down and intimate. Work these if you wish, but keep in mind what I have said.

Conventions.   Here's the fun crowd. These guys and gals are everything that the nightspot crowd is with one added feature: These people are hundreds of miles from home and ready to let themselves go. They consider the convention a tax deductible vacation. Even before you appear on stage they are happy, happy, *happy!* The only thing that might fail to go over will be ancient, moss-covered jokes. Give them funny, fresh material, insult them all you want, and involve them in the gags, and you will be successful and have fun doing it. Imagine being paid for entertaining such a fun group.

Pop concerts.   You will not appear at many of these, since comics are rarely used. But from time to time they gain an opening or front spot, or do a brief fill-in after intermission. This audience is not the best for the comic simply because they came to hear the musical group and see the big star. Don't turn these opportunities down, but don't expect to be a big hit.

Casino dining rooms and lounges.   These are actually two different audiences. The dining rooms feature name entertainers, but will often use a less known comic to open the show and warmup the audience. Try for these spots as soon as you feel you are ready. The customers are big spenders with full bellies, and having had a drink or two they make for a great audience. They expect professionalism, however, in both material and presentation. Let them down and you may also let your career down.

The casino lounge may be in the same building with the dining room, but the spectators' attitudes are at opposite poles. The lounge audience is in eyeshot and earshot of the gaming machines and tables, so their attention is divided. The sound of some guy hitting a jackpot just outside the lounge can induce them to leave you with a room full of empty tables. They really came to gamble after all, and you are just an extra feature thrown in. Casinos generally pay well and the working conditions are excellent, so you should be able to live with the one-armed bandit competition.

Shipboard audiences. Wouldn't you like to write a letter to some of your old school chums from the *Queen Elizabeth II,* or some other luxury liner where you are enjoying a cruise while being paid for it? These large liners hire good entertainers in the dancing, musical, comedy, and speciality areas, so make this one of your ambitions. You will dine superbly, live like royalty, and meet numerous influential people who can aid your career. The onboard audience is made up of genteel, polite, well-to-do highclass people. You will seldom, if ever, be heckled, and they will laugh at your routines. But some consider themselves qualified showbiz critics, and later among themselves will make caustic remarks about how stale your jokes were and how you bored them. But think about it: You are getting a cruise and a paycheck, so who cares?

By this point you will probably agree that audiences have separate and peculiar personalities, so much so that it is imperative that your comedic approach be appropriate for the type of audience you are to entertain.

Prior to Performance

While I have not exhausted existing audiences, this sample should suffice to convince you that every crowd can be a shade different in reaction from the last. With this in mind, the astute performer will see the importance of seeking out as much advance information about the audience as possible. When you have a personal manager, he or she will handle this duty for you. As a matter of fact, you can give your manager instructions as to which audiences you prefer and those before whom you will not appear under any circumstance. The manager can even have a clause inserted in your contracts that will forbid the serving of food during your performance. Don't get too demanding, however, until you are a widely known headliner.

Some of the advance information you might wish to know about the crowd would include ages, financial class, general occupational classification, level of education, and whether or not they are paying to see your performance. The size of the audience and the ratio of the sexes will also aid in determining just what course your routine should take, how long you should perform, and what special props might be used.

During the Performance

With time and experience, guaging your audience will come naturally. Despite all of the advance information you may have, you sometimes find yourself before a group unlike what you anticipated. And there will be times when full advance information is skimpy or nonexistent. One obvious yet often overlooked method of feeling them out is to have a series of test jokes with which to preface your act. One set may be political in nature, another pure corn, a third mildly risqué, and a fourth, if you get that far, bordering on the vulgar. By carefully listening to the audience reaction, you can then draw from your vast mental storehouse of jokes and give them the routine that you feel they will best enjoy.

Always carry with you a "spare tire," perhaps in the form of a comedy magic trick, a funny prop or two, and above all, a few guaranteed jokes that always get a laugh. As your career progresses you will come across about one of these special jokes per year, so keep them in a special file and always mentally handy so that you can drop them in as needed.

After the Performance

This may seem a little like pulling the plug after the fuse has blown, but it has a definite value. After each performance you should review the recording made while you were on stage or camera and listen specifically for audience reaction. Was it what you expected and anticipated? Did they laugh in the wrong places? Were there some groans? You will thus be programming your mind to be ultrasensitive to the audience's reception of your work and to better know, for future performances, what you did wrong and what you did right.

Conclusion

By now you are becoming more and more professional, for I have urged you into areas that amateurs either never consider important or simply never think about at all. Most amateurs see a comedian on television telling joke after joke into a microphone and are convinced that there is nothing more to it. It never occurs to them the amount of preparatory work that preceded that brief television appearance, but I sincerely want you to be a well-educated and well-prepared entertainer of whom the entire profession will be proud. So constantly evaluate your audiences in order that you may give them what they want: a million laughs. They, in turn, will give you what you want: a million dollars.

6

ON STAGE/
ON CAMERA

By now you have become introspective enough to determine whether or not you are naturally funny, and have reviewed the wide range of comedic activities available. You now know where comedy material originates. You have developed an awareness and concern for your appearance. You know the importance of analyzing your audiences so that you may more properly adapt to their cultural and intellectual levels. Sound like enough? Not at all. Important as they are, these activities are merely a prologue for the actual performance. It is now time for you to go onstage or on camera, so this chapter is devoted to alerting you to various areas often ignored by beginning comics. Let's talk about audience interplay, timing, adding music to your act, how to handle hecklers, and the use of cohorts.

Audience Interplay

One very effective comedy technique is to banter back and forth with members of the audience, drawing them into the act and thereby increasing their alertness. It is the same psychological effect that results in a classroom in which the instructor constantly pops questions to the students. You never know who will be called on next, and this produces nervous excitement. While the classroom students may more often than not feel uncomfortable, the audience members are well aware that their response or lack of it is not being graded and therefore they have nothing to lose. They recognize it as merely fun and games and will react accordingly.

One of the most obvious openings to begin audience interplay is the old, tired, wornout, yet surprisingly effective question, "Where are you from?" The performer can pick up on the answer by carrying it in any number of directions: a gag about small towns, a person's accent, a particular ball team, college, or large industry associated with that area, and so on. You get the idea. If the person mumbles, or is loud, or giggles, or hides her face, then the comic can play off of that to the embarrassment or glee of the victim and the delight of the rest of the audience. One comic did a twist on the "where are you from" routine. He said, "Let's save time. All of you shout out to me at the same time where you are from!" When the shouts died down, our supposedly astonished comedian gasped, "Is that right? Well, so am I!"

Actually inviting spectators onstage is the ultimate in audience participation. Comic magicians often do this with excellent results. One comic I knew would introduce his father and mother in the audience, then have them come onstage and stand there while he spewed forth an abundance of gags about his home life with them. It got laughs and no one in the audience ever suspected that they weren't his parents at all, but were hired actors.

While jokes and conversations with the audience members are commonly used, there are other techniques often employed with great success. Mixing in a bit of magic is a sure way to hold attention. Having audiences participate in a song will make them feel good and will result in making them receptive to whatever you offer next. And there is always the chance that during this bantering back and forth you may come up with a clown who is actually funnier than you. Use heckle stoppers if needed, but better yet, play on it for all it is worth.

"Dr." John Langley knows the value of drawing his audience into his act, even to the point of inviting Mary and Frank Taylor to join him on stage. (Photo courtesy of Carol Neal.)

Really milk it dry. That goofball may keep them entertained for your entire allotted time, and who gets paid for it? You do.

Some acts are solid audience interplay from start to finish. Others use it simply as an opener to put both the audience and the entertainer at ease. Then there are performers who never engage in any sort of dialogue with the spectators. Personally, I consider good-natured and witty audience teasing a most effective technique, but try it different ways with different audiences and find your own personal comfort zone in your continuing search for the biggest and longest laughs.

Timing

Give me someone who has no stage fright, who can make funny faces, who can costume up to get the guffaws and has a bag full of socko material, and if that person cannot master timing, I guarantee that he or she will fail as a comic. For some, it is the hardest of all traits to acquire, though it is absolutely the most essential. Give me the best joke in the world and I can murder it for you in seconds through bad timing.

Timing is simply the manner in which you deliver your material or actions. It is the ability to select, for maximum laughs, the precise moment for action or inaction. Pacing might be a more accurate word. If you pause too long, or if you run one thought into another with no pause, you are guilty of poor timing. Professional actors are masters of good pacing. Watch a serious professional drama on television or stage and note that it is far more than a recitation of lines. Those people interpret the written lines and deliver them in such a manner as to have you believe that they are originating all that is being said. They accompany the words with pauses, gestures, and facial expressions to the point that you accept them as the real participants of the drama, not merely actors. The same can be applied to comedy, but with a different approach. Quite often when a comic question is asked, it is far funnier if the answer does not come immediately. The comic pauses instead, perhaps widens his eyes in sudden realization of the situation behind the question, maybe twists his mouth, *then* delivers the answer which is heightened by his expert timing.

Does this come naturally? Can a person literally be born with a sense of timing? Yes. And you may be one of those people. If so, you are the exception and not the rule. Most entertainers cultivate this talent in two vital steps: They are acutely aware of the importance of pacing, and they study other entertainers who have mastered it and then practice what they observe.

I might add a third idea: Take a set of jokes or one liners at random. Video record yourself delivering these gems in various ways. Intentionally change your pacing several times for the same joke. This will drive home how easy it is to drain the life out of a perfectly good gag by imperfect delivery. Be your own critic and be tough on yourself. In addition, videotape your live performances whenever possible and review them until you can spot every flaw. Become determined that you will never make the same error again. Listen for audience reaction. If you thought you had a great joke but they didn't laugh, it is quite possible that it is your pacing, and not the joke, that is faulty.

Use of Music

This can often be the polish for your act. Many otherwise run-of-the-mill comedy routines have been saved by carefully chosen musical punctuation. If you work in a club or on a show that has a live band you have the ultimate situation, for the band members can give you your own theme song when you come on, rimshots where effective, piano arpeggios, laughing trombones, the necessary background for your rendering of a song, and chase music when you leave the stage. You are a real pro when you work with a live band. Maintain good relations with any musical group with whom you work, for they can make or break you.

The novice will more often than not work without the advantage of the live musical group. Overcoming the handicap is not difficult. By use of your fertile imagination and your mechanical ability, you can dub on audio tape your desired music, drumrolls, rimshots, and so on, and can actually control them on stage via a foot switch. *Voilá!* You have the next best

Want to learn the art of squelching hecklers fast? Just watch or listen to the famous Don Rickles. (Photo courtesy of Don Rickles.)

thing to the live band. You must of course observe all copyright laws and union rules governing such reproduction. In addition to or in place of the recorded music, you might display your own musical talent by having one or more instruments with you on stage to accompany your singing, stories, or gags. One young man attached bongo drums to his belt and gave himself rim-shots as needed.

Remember: Before dubbing music from existing recordings, be sure to let the record company know what you are doing. Seek their permission and ask if approval from others is also necessary.

Pantomiming recordings has already been mentioned in Chapter Two, so you might review that section now as you consider the best methods of employing music to polish your act. Music can put the finishing touch on your performance and make you a memorable entertainer. Use it discreetly and effectively, but use it.

How to Handle Hecklers

If I were a good liar I would assure you that all your audiences will be composed of pleasant, respectful people sitting with hands folded, laughing uproariously at your every line and gesture, then applauding wildly when you finish. That, I can truthfully confide to you, will not be the case. Audiences vary, as I have shown, depending on age groups, educational and cultural levels, and location. One sane individual when sober can change personality when drunk or on drugs, or (watch these rascals) when far away from home. Some of these will ignore you and continue with their loud boorish table conversation while you try to perform. Others will center their attention on you and offer a verbal barrage of garbage that will curl your hair. Most are not malicious. They simply want to get into the act, or, perhaps be the act. At any rate, these hecklers can make life miserable for the beginning comic.

Master heckle-stopper Bobby Lawson dares his audience to harass him. When people do, he tears 'em up. (Photo courtesy of Carol Neal.)

For the old pros, however, they are no match. The well-seasoned entertainer is sharply aware that the hecklers are out there and is prepared for them. Many comics build their acts around such kibitzers and are quite disappointed if there are none present.

The average audience loves nothing better than the comedian or M.C. putting hecklers down. You can always ignore hecklers, but generally this merely spurs them into livelier activity. Most comics have a mental reservoir filled to the brim with so-called squelchers or heckle stoppers. These are generally razor-sharp and barbed one liners designed to embarrass the person who is trying to embarrass or harass you. How many times have I enjoyed seeing a comic interrupt his patter to interpose: "If brains were money, this guy would be bankrupt!" Or, "Is that your nose, or are you eating a banana?" Want more? Here are a few that you might wish to add to your quickly growing repertoire of putdowns:

- "OK. So you *have* more hair than I do. After all, it's not what's on the *outside* of the skull that counts."
- "Why did you come in here, gal? Tired of street walking?"
- "And there he sits, ladies and gentlemen, the world's oldest living idiot."
- "She sounds like a real pro—the world's oldest."
- "What's your problem? Don't they give you enough attention at the nursing home?"
- "You, my dear, are a female dog."
- "Senility starts early in some people, doesn't it?"
- "You people sitting around her, look out. She sounds like she has a hairball."
- "Here's news for you, clown. The results of your IQ test just came in. Would you believe a minus twenty?"
- "I don't know what you're smoking, fella, but (slight pause) may I have some?"
- "And we wish to thank the representative from the local kindergarten for being with us tonight."
- "Who is that with you, sir, your wife or your dog?"
- "You have a voice that sounds like fingernails scratching a blackboard."
- "Howdy thar, podnah. You belong on the stage. And there's one leaving in half an hour. Make sure you're on it."
- "Is that a man or a woman back there? You sure can't tell by the voice."

These are given as examples and thought starters. You can easily write your own, though you may opt to purchase them from a professional writer. Memorize a supply of them and keep them on the tip of your tongue ready to spring forth when needed. The preceding examples are quite mild contrasted with the pointed, filthy, and bawdy slings that current comedians hurl at today's night club audiences. You may adjust your heckle stoppers to fit your crowd. Handle the situations as they arise, but don't ever let some inebriated clown take over your act. You are the star of the moment, so stand your ground. Ignore him if you can, but crucify him if you must.

Often a single comic will have numerous cohorts who aid in making his or her act successful. The audience could never guess how many people are involved in the planning of one performer's act. Above, comedian Ray Sauer plans a routine with confederates Evelyn Stanford, Maxine Street, Dawne Massey and Beth Sullivan. (Photo courtesy of Carol Neal.)

Use of Cohorts

A cohort is an accomplice. It is someone who works with you in the performance of your act but should not be confused with a partner. Partners work together and share equal billing. A cohort merely aids you while you are onstage or on camera, and may be a regular paid employee or someone you hire for a one-time shot. Occasionally you can get a volunteer, perhaps a member of the band, to aid you with one particular routine or sketch. This support widens your scope of comedic activity. It enables you to do things that simply cannot be effectively done by one individual, so never reject material or ideas simply because they require two or more people.

There are two types of cohorts, open and hidden. The open cohorts are actors who are obviously a part of your act. They appear from offstage to aid you or otherwise take part in your performance. They may merely produce props as needed or they may actually take part in a routine or sketch. They usually work as straightmen but may briefly step into the comedy spotlight while *you* become straightman for the moment.

While the open cohorts can embellish your act permitting you to accomplish comedic feats awkward or impossible for one individual, they can never equal the performance of hidden cohorts. These are performers placed in the audience who take the role of aggressive heckler or passive and innocent bystander, gradually being drawn into your act at your discretion. Many magic tricks owe their success to the use of hidden cohorts. When the great Charlie Chaplin was discovered, he was playing the part of a hidden cohort with Karno's Company, a traveling variety stage show out of England. He assumed the role of an inebriated member of the audience who steadily heckled each act, especially a staged boxing match. One of the huge boxers finally invited the little drunk on stage for fisticuffs. To the delight of the audience he stumbled from his theatrical box, made his way onstage, and engaged in a fantastically active routine with the resultant victory for the diminutive Charlie. Silent movie director Mack Sennett caught his performance and that is how Charlie Chaplin became a movie star.

How you use your hidden cohorts is limited only by your imagination. Suppose you are male and working a club with tables close to the stage or bandstand. You can easily place a shy young girl at a front table and start asking her embarrassing questions. If she is a good actress the audience will be completely taken in and royally entertained. Instead of the shy young girl, how about a sexy gal and her overly-jealous boyfriend, who is also an actor. Or consider an elderly gentleman or lady trading barbs with you. One idea often used to great humorous effect is to allow a waiter or waitress to go about their business until you bring them into your act either by trading insults or calling them onstage for a bit of nonsense. After all, twenty or thirty minutes of only one performer can become tedious, so adding cohorts brings variety and freshness to the act. Letting your cohorts literally get the best of you is often a good idea. The audience loves it.

Call them stooges, cohorts, or confederates, they make for good comic entertainment, and many famous partnerships began with one main character and his stooge. Volunteers may save you money, but they can't always be counted on to deliver the goods, and often their sense of timing is nonexistent. My advice is that you seek out and carefully screen your proposed cohorts and pay them well.

Conclusion

Perhaps you are beginning to realize that being a standup comic is not as simple as it has always seemed from the viewpoint of the spectator. You are right. The performance is the sum of many parts, each astutely blended with the other to produce an overall effect that is both pleasing and entertaining. The professional comic will have a mind trained to be aware of the importance of working with or playing off of the audience, and of the utter importance of timing. The comic must be able to juggle many techniques, including carefully chosen musical selections, a talent for handling hecklers, and the knowledge as to when and where a cohort can be brought into the act for embellishment.

7
STAGE FRIGHT

For every topflight comedic entertainer in the world, there are at least ten equally talented who never went beyond the first level of endeavor. Lack of education? Culturally deprived? Not at all. Instead they possessed a tragic flaw, an inner problem with which they could not cope, and it encircled them like a giant chain which held them down and literally pulled them under. That tragic flaw is stage fright. People who have never experienced it have no sympathy for nor empathy with people who suffer the sharp career destroying pangs of this most dreaded of show business maladies. To call it nervousness is totally inadequate. To call it mental illness would be closer to the truth. In reality there are no words to convey to the uninitiated the stark panic, dry mouth, palpitating heart, hyperventilation, and weakness that occur during an attack of stage fright. It is the ultimate in anxiety. It is a depressed feeling that something terrible is about to happen. It can be totally disabling. Some entertainers have it to a mild degree, while others go through hell. This chapter is a way of alerting you to the fact that, with effort, you can either conquer this bugaboo or learn to cope with it and move ahead with your career.

Lost Talent

During my high school and college days I knew a very talented young man who shared my sense of humor and entertained me royally. I can say without reservation that he was the funniest person I have ever seen, and I am including the greats of stage, television, and movies. At mimicry he was literally unsurpassed and could pantomime any given recording to the point of throwing me into hysterics. He was, at least in my mind, the funniest man alive. I could tell you his name, but you would not recognize it. I could show you his picture, but the face would be unknown. Despite my prodding and encouraging, he never entered show business. Why? Because of stage fright. With one or two people in the room, he could perform endlessly with impressions and exaggerated stories, keeping his friends in stitches. But I never saw him perform before a group. I never saw him on stage. The very thought petrified him. When it was suggested, you could see his strength and energy melt and his talent fade before your eyes. I honestly believe that had you given him a choice between picking up a rattlesnake or performing before an audience, he would have unhesitatingly reached for the former. Had I known then what I know now I could have helped him, but at that point all I could do was try to convince him that he would be all right as soon as he got onstage. He was convinced otherwise.

He never seemed to realize that I knew how he felt, for I also suffered nervous anxiety before and during performances. Even my wedding made me certain that I would never survive that ceremony. But I did go through with it (over thirty years ago) and have survived. Therein lies the difference between my talented friend and me. He surpassed me in talent but he lacked the desire and motivation to forge ahead in show business. I wanted the spotlight, applause, and public adulation so strongly that stage fright or no stage fright, I was going ahead.

Personal Experiences

One of my first paying jobs was as a comedy disc jockey on a large metropolitan area radio station. I was seventeen years old and knew pop music to the nth degree. I also had collected various sound effects, laugh and voice tracks, and knew that my show would go over. But here is how I spent the first week-and-a-half on that job. After a fitful night's sleep I would get up, shower, eat breakfast, ride my motor scooter to the radio station, where I would literally become physically ill, then go and prepare my show for the day. No, that was not just the first day. That was *every* day for the first week-and-a-half. By the time I got to the radio station each morning, I was so nervous and fearful that I literally became physically ill *every day*. But I was determined not to quit. Soon my nerves settled down. I became more familiar with the broadcast equipment, found myself making friends with other members of the staff and found success as a comedy DJ.

You would think that, since I had conquered it, it would never recur. But it did. That is a sad truth that I must impart to you. Stage fright can and will recur. Usually this happens at the opening of a new show or the beginning of a new show biz venture quite unlike what you have been doing. But it can happen suddenly right in the middle of an engagement with no perceptible change in circumstances or audience. It is, quite simply, a mental problem that is difficult to comprehend.

A few years later I found myself competing for the coveted Founder's Medal at Vanderbilt University. To win, I had to deliver a lengthy, original oration before a large audience. I had no trouble writing the speech and anticipated no problems while rehearsing—until the day of the contest. Suddenly that morning I became violently sick. I was nauseated, my hands shook, and I broke out in a cold sweat. My palms were wet but my mouth was as dry as cotton. I was too weak to stand, too nervous to lie down. I couldn't eat but knew that food was vital to have strength enough to stand on that podium in Alumni Hall that night when the three finalists would compete. In desperation I made my way to the Student Health Center and told the doctor my complete problem. He briefly counseled with me, gave me some tranquilizers, and admonished me to eat lightly and sleep in the afternoon if I could. I followed his directions and, thanks to the pills, slept for about three hours. Upon awakening I felt refreshed, ate a small supper and delivered my speech. I missed getting the Founder's Medal, but came in second. The stage fright did not really make me lose, for the first-place winner had a superior speech which was delivered far more dramatically than mine. He deserved to win.

But that night taught me something that I pass on to you because it is of vital importance to your future as an entertainer. I had to face the sad reality that I had weakened and used a drug (though prescribed) to make it through the contest. Without those pills I would have had to withdraw from the competition. Reflecting on this later I made up my mind that if I could not face an audience without using drugs for a crutch, then I would pursue some other line of work. The problem with drugs is that they can too easily become habit forming. Before you realize it they take over. The result can be total physical

Student comics can often aid each other in ridding themselves of stage fright before going in front of the crowd. Here, Thomas Brooks rehearses. (Photo courtesy of Carol Neal.)

and mental ruin, and success in show business will no longer be yours. If you don't believe me, talk to doctors in charge of drug rehabilitation centers. They can tell you horrible stories and show you sights that will burn in your memory forever. If it takes drugs to get you on stage, then you are compounding an already serious problem. There are better ways of handling the situation.

But to continue, I shall never forget my first night on stage in a burlesque house. I was scared witless, so I tried a device that I do not recommend: I crossed my eyes to make the audience a blur. Stupid? You bet. With the strong full set of footlights and the arc spot from the balcony, I couldn't have seen faces anyway. I came off stage with the world's number one headache, so I have never crossed my eyes since.

Slowly I came to realize that the best defense against stage fright is a good mental attitude toward the problem.

Conquering

Let's begin by implanting in your mind that your curse, disability, malefaction, or whatever you wish to term your distress at the thought of facing an audience, did not originate with you. You don't have a patent on it. You didn't discover it. The discomforting condition has probably been around since trilobites. You can take some degree of comfort in knowing that you share a camaraderie of sorts with your show business peers: Each of us has experienced stage fright to varying degrees. Any performer who claims that he or she has never had stage fright is a liar. So, my perspiring, shaking friend, there is nothing wrong with you. You will get over it or you will learn to live with it. Either way, it is all a part of paying your dues in order to be a professional entertainer. And the best news of all is that the strain that disturbs you is probably causing a flow of needed adrenaline that chemically aids you in performing far better than you might under calmer circumstances.

Have you ever heard the old gag about the comedian who quit show business because he just couldn't stand to be laughed at? We can reverse the gag and say that one reason for comics having stage fright is the fear of not being laughed at, which is simply fear of failing. This is a natural concern, since many people in your life are watching from the sidelines and hoping for your success. It would tear your heart out to fail, disappointing and letting them down. Your apprehension is understandable. But look at it this way: One blown performance is not failure. I knew an experienced comic who walked onto a Florida nightclub floor one night feeling panicky. He stared at the audience, then quietly informed them that he could not perform. Guess what? The audience shrugged it off. His boss was very understanding. No tidal wave destroyed Miami. There was no recorded earthquake. He returned the next evening and was a hit, and his career continues to this day. A few minor mishaps along the way will not matter in the long scheme of things. If you follow the directions in each chapter of this book and constantly seek guidance from more experienced comics, you will not fail in this business. So wipe the word failure out of your mind and concentrate only on those glorious rewards that success will bring you.

How about the comic starting out? One of your biggest problems is that your first audiences will probably be filled with people who know you well: friends, cousins, parents, brothers, sisters, uncles, aunts, and so on. Of course you have stage fright before these people. You will have to face everyone after the performance for the rest of your life. As soon as possible, divorce yourself from entertaining this group. Seek out audiences that don't know you, different schools, different churches, and civic clubs on the other side of town. Better yet, learn that travel is a part of this business and try for spots in nearby or distant communities. This way if your nervousness hampers your act, just shrug it off and go your merry way. In front of strangers chances are that you will not be nervous at all.

There is another odd psychological phenomenon connected with show business that you might wish to consider. Many people perform under names quite different from that with which they were born. And some say that when they made the change, their mental attitudes changed also. They feel that

One good way to conquer or cope with stage fright is to let yourself go. Be crazy! (Photo courtesy of Carol Neal.)

this new person is a personality separate and apart from themselves. They felt comfortable being in the company of the new person and never again had stage fright. Weird perhaps, but if the device works, use it.

I used to correspond with an elderly comedian who spent his early show business days in the United Kingdom. His lack of success at the beginning of his career so distressed him that he was willing to try almost anything to effect a positive change. One day he happened to realize that his name, Stan Jefferson, had thirteen letters. Though not superstitious, he decided to make an alteration just out of curiosity. He became *Stan Laurel* and his luck changed immediately. Later he joined a heavyset actor from Georgia named Oliver Hardy and they made numerous movies as the famous team of Laurel and Hardy.

As for the stage name you select, give it a great deal of thought for it can have a lot to do with your success, or lack of it.

A name that is not crisp and fresh may not come across well on television. People won't be able to remember you, so strive for a name that can be easily pronounced and understood. Catchy names should not be overlooked. I recently analyzed the names of fifty-three living comics, chosen randomly, to show you that shorter names are definitely preferred. As for first names, only one of the fifty-three had three syllables; twenty-five had two syllables; and twenty-seven had only one syllable. As for the last names, only two had three syllables; forty had two syllables; and eleven had only one syllable. Following are a few showbusiness names, followed in parentheses by their real names:

- *Woody Allen* (Allen Stewart Konigsberg)
- *Orson Bean* (Dallas F. Burrows)
- *Milton Berle* (Milton Berlinger)
- *Joey Bishop* (Joseph A. Gottlieb)
- *Red Buttons* (Aaron Chwatt)
- *Cheech & Chong* (Richard Marin & Tommy Chong)
- *Redd Foxx* (John Elroy Sanford)
- *Buddy Hackett* (Leonard Hacker)
- *Alan King* (Irwin Alan Kniberg)
- *Jackie Mason* (Yacov Moshe Maza)
- *Mike Nichols* (Michael Igor Peschowsky)
- *Joan Rivers* (Joan Molinsky)
- *Danny Thomas* (Amos Jacobs)
- *Flip Wilson* (Clerow Wilson)

I have personally worked under more names than I can remember, a practice I advise against since success can come only to an established identity. Most of my chosen titles were corruptions of my real name (Kenneth Berryhill), though some were totally different: Ken Hill, Barry Hill, Ken Barry, Jerry Macon, Dr. Dunker, Ken, Boo-Boo the Clown, and so forth. I even worked as Benny Hill until I discovered that an English actor/comedian had the name before I did. As for the assumed identities aiding in the alleviation of my stage fright, I can truthfully say that they did, for if the new character failed all I had to do was drop the name and assume a new one. Furthermore, I seemed to feel that the character was a separate personality, another person for whom my feelings were, at best, objective. Early in your career you just might want to work under a different name. Give it serious consideration.

In addition to or instead of changing your name as a method of conquering stage fright, you might develop a sense of bravado, an attitude that combines bravery with an air of "Who cares?" thrown in. This feeling can carry you over many rough spots if you can expand it fully. You can instill it into your character by concentrated effort over a period of time. You might ask yourself, "If I get stage fright, what is the worst that can happen to me?" The answer is: You will die. In over fifty years, however, I have yet to see anyone die of stage fright. If your symptoms are severe, I would advise that you go for a complete physical examination, telling your physician of the strain you are under while performing. If he or she checks you over carefully (including your heart) and gives you the go-ahead, stop worrying about dying from stage fright. It is not going to happen. Just convince yourself that this is a normal discomfort that will pass, and keeping going.

Coping

Like myself, many performers have never been able to fully conquer this malady. We have learned to cope with it, and when possible, use it to our advantage. One trick I have used successfully is self-hypnosis. I used to laugh at the idea until I tried it before a trip to the dentist, and it worked. One way to do it is to stand in front of a mirror and look intently into your eyes. Talk softly to yourself, rationalizing the entire situation that is bothering you. Then convince yourself that you can easily survive any discomfort or disturbance that may soon beset you. Never tell yourself there will be no uncomfortable feelings and no anxiety, because this will be contrary to actuality. Convince yourself instead to rest easy in the knowledge that you are strong enough to take any storm and that it will only hurt for a little while. Keep it up until you feel relaxed and confident. The secret to it, I suppose, is the inability to lie to oneself.

Another approach is the security blanket or witch doctor method. Take with you onstage some good luck object. It can be very small and carried in your pocket, or it can be a good luck piece of your costume. It might be a prop of some kind. It could even be a musical instrument. Almost anything can act as a psychological support, so if it gives you pleasure, use it.

My favorite procedure for coping with stage fright is to always leave myself an out. By this I mean that I will make every effort to perform, but only with the understanding that I can, at any given point, withdraw from the action. Here is how it can work for you. Suppose that your fear is so pronounced that it has literally put you to bed. Begin by making a very minor decision, not a major one. Decide to see if you can stand. Once you accomplish that, see if you can walk to the door without suffering an apoplectic seizure. To your amazement, you will be able to do it. Now, another decision: Take a shower. OK so far? Then decide to drive to the comedy showcase. You haven't decided yet that you will appear on the show. All you want to do is see if you can drive there with the understanding that you can stop and return home at any moment that fear dictates. Once you are there, make a decision to walk to the stage entrance just to see what will happen. Remember that even in the company of the other members of the show, you reserve the right to back out whenever you wish. I have performed more shows than you would believe using this seemingly naïve and childish philosophy. Just take it one step at a time and always leave yourself an out.

One trick used by thespians for many years is to take three deep breaths just before going on stage. The secret here, I suppose, is the resulting lightheadedness caused by the sudden introduction of oxygen to the brain. Whatever the physiological ramifications, I have tried it and found it effective in relieving tension.

The best overall defense against stage fright is to stay in perfect mental and physical health at all times. Constantly study recent books on nutrition. Eat sensibly, drink plenty of water, exercise moderately but regularly, and sleep well. When you feel good and have steady nerves, you can handle virtually any problem. You have a feeling of self-confidence and well-being.

Perhaps the best way to build confidence and self-assurance is extensive rehearsing. You may practice with others if you like, but I consider solitude best for the one person act. Go over your material just as you would deliver it before the audience, even pausing for laughter. If you are to be on television, put two or three white or red spots at eye level in the room to simulate camera *on the air* lights, and practice looking directly into and occasionally changing cameras. You cannot rehearse too much. Take breaks as necessary, but get back to it. After a while it becomes so ingrained in you that it flows automatically, and that is what will happen on stage. You will perform involuntarily and stage fright will probably never enter your mind.

Finally, here is a method of coping with the problem that appeals to me, though I have never used it. Go before the assemblage admitting that you suffer from stage fright. Ask for their sympathy or chide them for their lack of it. Have a series of stage fright jokes ready. I have seen this used a few times, and while it may not have done much for the audience, it certainly worked wonders for the performers. The comics in question calmed down immediately and continued their routines with cool, calculated aplomb.

Conclusion

Since you share this disabling disorder with other entertainers, why not seek them out and ask their experiences and techniques for handling the problem. A shared distress is immediately tempered. I have often wondered why someone does not organize a Stage Fright Anonymous Club. Its membership, surely, would be almost equal to the population of the entire world.

Be concerned about the problem of stage fright, but do not

let it slow you down one bit. Do whatever it takes to mitigate the suffering, short of taking drugs, and forge ahead. Before a performance take a shower, jog, get a massage, rest, or listen to music. Keep trying various ideas until you hit upon the one that works for you. Remember that a great part of stage fright is merely normal excitement that will actually enhance your act. Try to look upon the problem as something to be lived with and used to your advantage.

8
BEING FUNNY FOR MONEY

W_e come now to the crucial point of getting jobs. An unemployed comic is not funny. I would like to inch you into your first amateur appearances, then segué you into the wonderful world of professional entertaining where you are paid for having fun. Advantages of booking agents and personal business managers will be covered as will unions and the monetary compensation to be expected in later years.

You are now ready to be funny for money.

Beginning

The novice comic may feel confident about his or her act, yet reticent about approaching someone about performing, especially for pay. While meteoric careers are often touted, they seldom happen. The best advice is to enter show business quietly and without fanfare until you build up both your poise and your portfolio.

The absolute first step, after you have digested all that I

have told you in the previous chapters, is to simply get on stage before an audience. Don't worry about where it is, audience size, or whether or not you are paid. Your first few jobs will more than likely be gratis.

Your school or college is an excellent launching pad. During the year, numerous plays and variety shows will be presented, and you should seek out the person in charge and ask to audition. This will teach you what rejection feels like, as many of these shows are somewhat exclusive. Don't be discouraged. Sooner or later someone will give you a chance, and whether you go over big or not that first time does not matter. What is significant is that you get the feel of going before the crowd, doing your bit, and hearing the reaction. I don't have to tell you to seek a second show, because by this time you will be hopelessly hooked.

Don't ever lose sight of the fact that you are not appearing before the best and most objective audience when you perform in your school or college. These people know you too well and will have difficulty accepting you as the character you portray, but it is still a good place to simply get onstage or on camera and try your wings.

Another equally easy place to begin is in churches. They welcome local entertainers, especially those who work free. Don't let the fact that it is a freebie deter you. What you want at this juncture is experience, and shows like this will give it to you.

There are other organizations in your community that offer a chance for the novice: civic and garden clubs, military veterans' clubs, and large business concerns which regularly hold meetings for employees, to mention only a few.

Here is how to approach these people. Let's say that you wish to appear at the Goodhaven Retirement Home. Look up the phone number of the Home, dial, and ask to speak to the person in charge of entertainment. They may merely take your number. If this happens and a week goes by and they haven't returned your call, call again. Be persistent, but never obnoxious. When you finally get the person you desire, be prepared to describe your act in a few words, adding that you perform free for nonprofit organizations. The chances are great that no audition will be necessary. You will probably be booked for the next show then and there.

With these free shows it is always important that you get permission to announce to the audience, either via the M.C. or yourself, that you *are* available for shows and parties. And have a sheet or card available that has your name, type of act, and phone number. This way, freebies can lead directly to paying jobs. Calls will not come fast at first, but they will come if you aggressively work at getting before the public and publicizing your act.

News Releases

In addition to advertising your act when you perform, you should also be your own press agent and make sure that the local media gets a news release about your appearance well in advance of the performance date. You might even mention that photographers and reporters are welcome. Until you fully establish your show business identity, most of these releases will never appear in print or on radio or TV. But you are helping to make a name for yourself with every release, because somebody will read each and every one. The release may hit the wastebasket, but your name will stick in someone's mind. Sooner or later the media will publish your release as written or give you a call and request an interview, or appear at your performance with a camera.

Here are a few brief tips about sending your own news releases:

1. At the top of the page (and on the envelope) type NEWS RELEASE in capital letters.
2. Date the release.
3. Indicate FOR IMMEDIATE RELEASE in capital letters or put a specific release date if the announcement is to be held until a particular date.
4. Beneath the release date type the word LEAD with a colon after it, followed by the subject of the release. This permits the re-

porter or editor to see at a glance what it is about without reading the entire announcement.

5. Below the LEAD, type "For Additional Information Call . . ." followed by the name and phone number of the person who can provide any other facts about you, your act, or the show in which you are appearing.

An even bolder approach is to call the media directly and offer yourself for an interview, special feature, article, or program. Be prepared to provide black and white glossy photographs if they are desired. Is this being too presumptuous? Not at all. As a matter of fact, you are doing their job for them. They need new material daily and seek out features on personalities constantly. You will be walking in with a ready-made article. You do the work, you get your name before the public, they get credit for it, and everybody's happy.

Portfolio

As these news releases appear, diligently clip and save several copies. When you appear on television make sure that a photo is taken of you on the set or of the television screen itself. While photos of TV screens are seldom the best quality, they are dramatic, and they highlight the fact that you were on the air. Make sure that you have signed permission from all parties involved, letting them know your intended use of the photographs. Also keep a list of every appearance you make onstage or on camera, whether performing your comedy act or being interviewed. Eventually, when you become professional, you will want to incorporate all of this into a book or portfolio which can be used in acquiring future jobs. This dossier will be modified and updated numerous times over the years as you insert new material and withdraw dog-eared or faded clippings. Keep it neat and uncluttered. Plan each page with care. It is not a scrapbook. It is a sales presentation, so assume the role of the person viewing it and design it with that person's considerations in mind.

Brochure

When you become professional you will want to design, or have designed, a suitable handout or mailing piece. This will contain two or three black and white glossy photos of you in varied poses, plus concise yet complete information about you, your act, and your credits. It will also include your agent's name, address, and phone number (including area code). If all contacts should be made through your manager, then his or her information would replace the agent's. You might in rare cases wish to list both names. Discuss this with both your manager and booking agent. They will aid you in the overall design of the brochure or will, at your direction and approval, completely take over responsibility for its design and printing. It is a most important tool in the business since many of the people hiring you will never actually have personal contact with you. What they read and see in the brochure must be appealing and complete.

Applying for Jobs

Before you reach the level of having an agent and personal manager you will be responsible for booking yourself. While your approach and technique will vary with each potential job, here are a few brief hints to help you get started.

Decide early the very least amount of money you will perform for, and make it a hard and fast rule to never, under any circumstances, work for less. Some employers will offer a set fee, take it or leave it, so be prepared to do just that. Some will ask your fee. In this case never give your minimum figure first; always start higher. Then be prepared to come down if you see that you have no choice. There are others who will want an indication of your charge and you may ask, "What is your offer?" You are hoping here, of course, for a high figure. Whatever the answer, you are in position to accept, refuse, or bargain.

Berkeley Davis is a burst of energy when she goes on stage. She never refuses an opportunity to perform. (Photo courtesy of Carol Neal.)

By watching newspaper and television ads as well as outdoor notices, you will soon make a list of area locations that either regularly or periodically employ entertainers. For example, you may see a television news story about a big outdoor, Fourth of July variety show held the afternoon before. Even if it's too late to consider for this year, you can make a note to begin your efforts in March or April to be on next year's show. And here's a tip: Most places that hire bands will also hire comics. If you pass a place and the marquee features a band, put that on your list as a potential job. When you go into a place of business or call on the phone seeking an interview with the director of a show, make sure that you are talking to the person who can and will make the decisions. Few things are more frustrating than going through an entire sales pitch only to find out that you have been talking to the wrong individual. And at times that wrong person will take it upon himself to reject you.

Keep precise records on every job in one of the following forms: index cards, large file, journal, or computer. Your information should include the date, place of business, contact person, and results.

Auditions

Now and then you will be asked to audition, so be prepared. Don't go in with the idea of performing your entire act. Give instead a representative sampling of your choicest material. If they want to see the complete routine, then let them see it.

And be warned that auditions are usually held in less than favorable circumstances. I once auditioned while an electronics engineer was repairing the PA (public-address system), so I worked without a mike (microphone). At another audition I gave a sample performance while a chorus of tap dancers practiced behind the curtain. In situations like this, change the time, date, or place if you can. If not, forge ahead and do your best no matter what. Whatever you do, wear makeup and costume for the audition and use your regular props. Through my influence I recently got a friend a tryout on a national cable network. She went to the studio with the idea that she had plenty of time to put the costume and makeup on. She was

The famous Pidge incorporates jokes about his diminutive size into his routine, but he basically relies on current events to keep his monologues fresh. His career began at the famous Clown College in Venice, Florida. (Photo courtesy of Carol Neal.)

wrong. They immediately put her before the cameras and told her to do her stuff. The audition was a failure.

One major problem with auditions is that the lighting is either improper or nonexistent. Always make an effort to have good lighting by requesting it in advance. If nothing else, one simple spotlight will help and may make the difference between getting the job or losing it.

Some Good Advice

If you owned a business, would you be likely to hire someone who came in and said, "I'm not very good, but will you hire me?" That negative attitude is unappealing to any employer. When you decide that you are ready to become a professional and accept money for your act, don't ever represent yourself as an inexperienced amateur just hanging around the edges of show business for kicks. If you are a professional, act like one. Show your experience, not your lack of it. Be businesslike. Let them know that you are competent and self-assured. Let your demeanor indicate that you know how to do a good job for them by pleasing audiences night after night.

Is an Agent Really Necessary?

Yes. I never really felt like a professional until I signed up with an entertainment bureau. These people find jobs for you. You may be represented by several people, but more likely you will be assigned to one particular agent who will learn all about you and your act. That person will watch your performance and decide with you on the best way to market your routine and your special brand of humor. These agencies have their fingers on the pulse of show business and have contacts of long standing who call them constantly for acts, so they are already set up to do what would take you years to accomplish. You will pay them a percentage of what you make from the jobs they book you into, and they earn their money.

Contracts with booking agents can vary, so read yours carefully. Show it to an attorney before signing if you have any reason to believe that the terms displayed may be unfair. Their proffered contract is not written in stone, so you have the right to negotiate and make changes that are mutually agreeable. Even though most of these contracts are standard, read the terms carefully before signing. Some newcomers to the business prefer nonexclusive contracts which permit them to get bookings on their own at the same time the agency is handling them. While this may sound like the smart thing to do, it can cause confusion and mistrust and at times can discourage the agent from putting forth full effort. Look an agency over very carefully and ask their former and present clients about them, and sign on an exclusive basis when you feel that the time is right. Even then I would not enter into long-term contracts early in your career. Go for one year at first. If all works out, extend the time period. And as for having no contract and merely working together from a handshake, that is stupid beyond words. It can, and often does, end in financial disaster for one or both of you. Ask any attorney.

Is a Personal Manager Really Necessary?

Let me first explain the difference between your booking agent and your manager. The booking agent is a sales representative who seeks out entertainment job opportunities, does all of the negotiating, and books you in. He or she may represent many entertainers. Some specialize and represent only comics, or singers, or actors.

A personal or business manager will handle all of your business affairs outside of booking. The manager will deal directly with the booking agent for you and control all details, including transportation and hotels for booked engagements. Unlike the booking agent the manager will not represent numerous entertainers, but will instead handle very few per- formers at one time. While standard contracts exist, it is usu- ally a matter of the entertainer and the manager making a list of what the latter will do for the former, deciding on the length of the contract, and determining what percentage of the gross income the manager will receive. Final wording should be handled by an attorney.

With all of these percentages going out of your gross in- come, one might wonder if there will be any net income. Look at it this way: These paid percentages are business expenses and are tax deductible. You are in effect deciding to pay the money to the people who work for you rather than paying it to the government. Believe me, whatever they make they deserve, and they have every incentive to aid and instruct you in a manner to raise both your professional standing and your in- come. When you make more, they make more.

Duties of the manager can be very broad or extremely restrictive. It is up to you. Often he or she literally manages all of your money, including investments, preparation of income tax returns, and payment of said tax. That person might also

Pidge receives advice from the author concerning the delivery of some new comedy material. (Photo courtesy of Carol Neal.)

take over all phone calls and correspondence which, after you become a star, can grow to become unmanageable. While we all love our fans and want more of them, they can unintentionally cause problems from time to time, especially when we are on tight schedules and have experienced loss of sleep. Here the manager can step in and deal with them, keeping the fans happy while letting you rest. Furthermore, the monumental task of sending press releases, planning interviews, and notifying the media can be handled by your personal business manager. Whatever the two of you agree on will be in the contract.

Keep in mind that both the booking agent and the manager are busy people, so don't call them everyday asking if they have anything for you. This will drive them to distraction and their efforts on your behalf might slacken. How often and in what manner they are to be contacted is a matter to be discussed when contracts are drawn up and periodically reviewed. Even if one says, "Feel free to call me anytime," he or she will probably regret having said it if you constantly phone. Hold back. Let them call you. Then, from time to time, make a very quick phone contact, drop by briefly, or drop a note in the mail. Informally yet concisely, don't bug them.

Is Union Membership Necessary?

The answer is no while you are still an amateur doing your act for free around your hometown. But when you become a serious professional, the answer is yes.

The decision as to which union to join will be based on what area of show business you end up in, and many people join more than one. A man might be a comic and a musician who takes serious acting roles. He might have reason to join two or more unions. Unions have distinct advantages for their members, but before joining read all of their material so that you will fully understand what they stand for and in what ways they can advance your career.

Many states have open shop laws, meaning that in those states one cannot be denied a job if not a union member. Regardless of this fact, you will probably travel from state to state in your work, so union membership will be to your professional advantage.

The beginning comic who plans to work comedy stores, showcases and club dates need not join a union, though he/she should investigate the advantages of affiliating with the American Guild of Variety Artists.

If music is incorporated into the act, whether playing an instrument or utilizing approved recorded music, I suggest that you join the American Federation of Musicians. Cities of any size will have a local chapter listed in the Yellow Pages under "labor organizations" and/or "associations." The listing may read: "(name of city) Federation of Musicians, which will be the title of the local chapter. Membership in one is recognized by all other chapters.

The time will come when you will begin to make radio and television appearances, and at that time you should apply for membership in AFTRA (American Federation of Television and Radio Artists) and/or SAG (Screen Actors Guild). Your talents may be utilized in these mediums for talk shows, commercials, movies or brief comedy inserts. The ultimate will be your own television show. For movie parts, membership in SAG will be essential. This union is not open to everyone who walks in off of the street, so your manager will aid you in procuring membership in this august body of entertainers. It is a large and powerful labor force and I cannot emphasize too strongly the obvious advantages of your affiliation.

Since both SAG and AFTRA involve those working in television, you and your manager should contact each association to determine whether you should join just one, or both. Representatives of each group will be happy to discuss your chosen areas of endeavor, your career in general and how their organization might be of benefit to you.

Does Comedy Pay Well?

When you hit the big time, you bet comedy pays well. The only reason I hesitate to include many salary figures is that within a year or two they will have changed—upward. Let's put it this way: How would you like to earn, just for telling jokes, between $200,000 and $500,000 per week? Sounds unbelievable, I know, but it is true. Over $200,000 per week. That is a goal worth striving for. I am, of course, talking about the *big* time, the absolute top spots in Las Vegas, Atlantic City, and in the best resort hotels and theaters. Below that, the pay scale comes down. But even at its worst it generally pays far more than just a comfortable living. If you are a talented, fulltime, dedicated comic with a good personal business manager and an established booking agency, you soon could be driving a Mercedes-Benz, Cadillac, Lamborghini, BMW, or Maserati and will be enjoying weekends on your sailboat.

Your job is to bring paying customers in. The more who come to see you, the more money your backers will make. The more they make, the more they will pay you. It really is that simple.

To the beginners' advantage are the numerous showcase clubs that dot the country, catering to comedy performers only. They have amateur nights, but they also book in headliners who earn up to $1,500 working only four nights (sometimes three) a week. Pay for those of lesser status is far lower and can be as far down as $10 to $35 per performance. Keep in mind that what is earned, however, is not as important as how much is saved and astutely invested from your net income. There are tax shelters available and you should invest very conservatively, holding back on highly speculative investments until you have money that, if lost, won't destroy you. Here is where a good personal business manager comes in. His or her guidance can be invaluable.

Conclusion

May I make a prediction? You will someday be a topflight, headlining, comic entertainer. I am *certain* of it. How could I possibly know? Simply because you are reading these words right now. You see, the intellectually deficient, half-interested potential comic, who thought that it was all so easy and desired show business merely as an affectation, stopped reading about four chapters back. But you, with your ability to comprehend and perceive so clearly and with your burning desire to succeed at whatever you set out to do will succeed beyond your most exorbitant expectations. I know that you will be unique and original and will nurture your show business contacts. You will move to the top of the profession, and you will stay there because you believe in me and will follow the directions in this book faithfully. In spirit I will be with you on stage and in the audience, laughing and applauding, with perhaps a tear glistening in one eye for I'll be proud of you beyond words. There is an affinity between us now, and it will last as long as either of us can give forth a snappy one liner.

Before parting, may I ask a favor? In return for what I have given you through this book, will you in turn seek to aid some other novice who has talent and intelligence but needs a guiding hand?

INDEX

A

Adkins, Jack, 4, 6, 10
AFTRA (American Federation of
    Television and Radio Artists),
    122
Agent, 118–19
Allen, Woody, 63, 104
American Federation of Musicians,
    122
American Federation of Television
    and Radio Artists (AFTRA), 122
American Guild of Variety Artists,
    122
Amsterdam, Morey, 63
Applying for jobs, 111–13, 114–18
Audiences:
    gauging, 78–80
    hecklers, 88–90
    interplay, 83–85
    types, 72–78
Auditions, 117–18

B

Bean, Orson, 104

Berle, Milton, 104
Berman, Shelley, 63
Bishop, Joey, 104
Blue material, 44–45
Bob and Ray, 13
Booking agencies, 118–19
Brenner, David, 75
Brochure, 115
Brooks, Thomas, 100
Burlesque, 9
Business manager, 119–21
Buttons, Red, 104

C

Carlin, George, 60
Chaplin, Charlie, 60, 92
Cheech and Chong, 104
Chong, Tommy, 104
Clichés, 43
Clown, 9, 17–19
Clown College, 117
Cohorts, 91–93
Combination performer, 28–29
Comedy material:
    borrowed/stolen, 34–36

Comedy material (*cont'd*)
  filing, 45–46
  library, 43
  memorizing, 46–50
  obscene, 44–45
  original, 37–41
  purchased, 41–43
Conway, Tim, 13
Costume, 60

D

Davis, Berkeley, 116
Diller, Phyllis, xi–xii, 63, 74
Dossier, 114

E

Elliott, Bob, 13

F

Farce, 9
Fields, Lew, 7
Ford, Gerald R., 42
Foxx, Redd, 104

G

Gallagher and Shean, 7
Gallagher, Ed, 7
Goulding, Ray, 13
Gregory, Dick, 40

H

Hackett, Buddy, 13, 104
Hardy, Oliver, 12, 103
Hecklers, 88–90
Hill, Benny, 104
Humor:
  comparison and contrast, 9
  hyperbole (exaggeration), 8
  joke, 7
  repetition, 8–9
  of situation, 8
  spoonerism, 8
  of words, 8

I

Impressionist, 10, 24–25
Irony, 10

J

Jargon, 43
Jokes (*see* Comedy material)
Juggler, 27–28

K

Keystone Kops, 57
King, Alan, 104

L

Labor organizations, 122
Langley, "Dr." John, 13, 62, 85
Laurel and Hardy, 12, 103
Laurel, Stan, 12, 13, 103
Lawson, Bobby, 27, 29, 89
Length of routine, 50

M

Magician, 26–27
Makeup, 55–60
Manager, 119–21
Marin, Richard, 104
Martin, Steve, 13, 61
Martindale, Wink, 25
Mason, Jackie, 104
Massey, Dawne, 23, 91
Master of Ceremonies, 25–26
Material (*see* Comedy material)
M. C. (Master of Ceremonies), 25–26
Meara, Anne, 72
Memorizing, 46–50
Mimicry, 10
Music, 87–88

N

Name change, 102–5
Neal, Carol (photographs by), 4, 6, 10, 13, 23, 27, 29, 39, 44, 56, 59, 61–63, 65, 85, 89, 91, 100, 103, 116–17, 120

News releases, 113–14
Nichols, Mike, 104

O

Orben, Robert, 40–42
Organic attention, 19

P

Paar, Jack, 40
Pantomime:
    recordings, 10, 20–21, 64
    silent, 19–20
Parody, 10
Pay scale, 122–23
Pidge (Eugene J. Pidgeon, Jr.), 56,
    117, 120
Pidgeon, Eugene J., Jr., 56, 117, 120
Portfolio, 114
Props, 62–67

R

Rickles, Don, 87
Ringling Brothers, Barnum & Bailey
    Circus, 56
Ritz Brothers, 13
Rivers, Joan, 104
Ross, Ken (photography by), 66
Routine:
    length, 50
    memorizing, 46–50

S

SAG (Screen Actors Guild), 122
Sarcasm, 10–11
Satire, 11
Sauer, Ray, 23, 91
Schenck, Joe, 7
Screen Actors Guild (SAG), 122
Seinfeld, Jerry, 34
Sennett, Mack, 92
Shean, Al, 7
Skelton, Red, 13, 40

Sketch performer, 23
Slapstick, 9
Stage fright, 97–108
Stage name, 102–5
Standup comic, 21–23
Stanford, Evelyn, 23, 91
Stewart, Cal (Uncle Josh), 7
Stiller and Meara, 72
Stiller, Jerry, 72
Street, Maxine, 91
Sullivan, Beth, 91

T

Taylor, Rip, 13
Thomas, Danny, 38, 104
Thomas, Richard, 58
Timing, 85
Tucker, John Bartholomew, 24

U

Uncle Josh (Cal Stewart), 7
Union membership, 121–22

V

Van and Schenck, 7
Van, Gus, 7
Vulgarity, 44–45

W

Weber, Joe, 7
Weber and Fields, 7
Williams, Bert, 7
Williams, Dot, 59, 61, 63, 66
Williams, Robin, 13
Wills, Nat M., 7
Wilson, Flip, 104
Wit, 11
Wright, Steven, 36

Y

Youngman, Henny, 63